The Captain's Craps Revolution

Stand your ground....if they mean to have war let it begin here!

...John Parker

The
Captain's
Craps
Revolution

by

Frank Scoblete

Paone Press

(c) **1993, 1995 by Paone Press**

ISBN 1 - 882173 - 03 - 1

Printed in the United States of America

Paone Press
PO Box 610
Lynbrook, NY   11563

*This book is dedicated
to
Mr. and Mrs. Sal D'Amato,
for their class and understanding,*

and

*To the Memory
of
Russ Barracca and Frank Torre,
who are sorely missed by the Captain and Crew*

Contents:

Acknowledgments

No book writes itself and no author is an island, to paraphrase John Donne. So let me thank the people who have made the creation of this book possible. To my editors at Paone Press: the delightful A.P., and the ever reasonable Albert Ross; to Howard T. Mann, who does a lot of running around for me; to John F. Julian, who reviewed the manuscript and suggested some telling and intelligent cuts; to Dorothy Kavka, for being so competent, talented, and pleasant; to Alan Tinker for his insights into the *5-Count*. Of course, the biggest thanks is reserved for the Captain himself for letting me write about him and his methods with no strings attached. And last on my thank you list but first in my heart, to my sons Greg and Mike, whose love keeps me plugging away at my word processor - to pay for their tuition!

I have set my life upon a cast,
And I will stand the hazard of the die.

...*Richard III* by William Shakespeare

Chapter One

The Captain, Craps, and You

Some people hate me. I am not a hateful guy but nevertheless I'm hated.

One boxman at Binions Horseshoe in downtown Las Vegas had this to say about me when he saw me and my good friend Alan Tinker playing the Supersystem: "Look at them!" said the boxman. "No one should be allowed to play that way! Ever since that book! Whoever wrote that book should be killed! This is ridiculous. That stupid book! The guy who wrote that book should be hanged."

Thankfully, the boxman did not know I was the author of the infamous book in question. He looked fully capable of putting his threats into action.

At the Tropicana in Las Vegas a dealer had similar thoughts when he saw me and the lovely A.P. playing the Supersystem.

"You know that's like cheating," he said to us.

"What do you mean?" I said.

"It's like cheating, the way you play," he said.

"I'm not cheating," I said. "I'm just playing a smart game."

"It shouldn't be allowed," said the dealer.

I guess some casinos just expect you to walk in and hand over your money, thinking that you are overjoyed that they have allowed you to play.

At the Frontier in Las Vegas, a very nice dealer said to me: "You're playing that new way, too?"

"Are a lot of people playing this way?" I asked.

"We're seeing some, yes. Can't figure it out though. When you bet, when you don't bet. What's the formula?"

"I read it in a book," I said, not wanting to tell him I had written the book. Two other people at the table were also playing the Supersystem, and one even had a copy of the book in his back pocket! I was hoping he wouldn't recognize me from my picture on the back cover. Who knew? Maybe the *Frontier* wanted to hang the author of that book, too.

"I think a lot of people have read the book," he said.

"You don't like having to deal with these bets?" I asked.

"Not at all. It's bothering them," he said and pointed behind him to the suits in the pit. "You guys are cutting into our profits playing this way."

Bob, the owner of the limo service I use, is a former crazy crapper - a guy who used to make all the proposition bets. He is one of the most exuberant and enthusiastic craps players I've ever met and he now plays the Supersystem with almost religious fervor.

Bob relates this tale that occurred to him at the Foxwoods casino in Connecticut.

"I was playing the Supersystem and everyone was sevening out within the *5-Count.* So I really hadn't lost anything because I had not as yet placed any money at risk. This young dealer, a nice kid, said to me: 'Sir, you can't win that way!' I jokingly said to him: 'Oh, I don't want to win, I just want to hang around!' An hour later, I was up $400 and I turned to him and said: 'How am I doing?' The dealer shook his head and said: 'How did you win? This table's been ice cold.'"

At Tropworld, currently the best craps game in Atlantic City, one pit boss told a high-roller friend of mine who was playing the Supersystem: "I'm sorry, sir, we aren't going to be able to rate your play today." When the high roller asked why, the pit boss hemmed and hawed. Finally, the high roller pressed him for an explanation and the pit boss responded: "Frankly, playing that new way, we don't have much of an edge on you. You'll be taking our comps but more than likely we won't be taking your money."

Don't feel sorry for the casinos, they'll be taking plenty of other people's money.

At the Claridge, another quite friendly dealer tried to explain to me that he would be more than happy to make *place* bets for me. When I told him that I preferred to play the way I was playing, he just shrugged. Then the pit boss came over to him.

"Did you tell him? Did you tell him?" asked the pit boss of the dealer.

"Yes," said the dealer.

Then the pit boss leaned over to me. "You know," he said, "the dealers can place you on any number you want. You'll go directly up on the number. You can also pull off anytime you want."

"Thanks," I said, "but I like to play this way."

When the pit boss left, I turned to the dealer. "He seemed pretty insistent."

"We've been told to offer other bets for people who play as you do. They want us to push place betting for you. They think it's better betting."

"For who?"

"That's a good question," laughed the dealer.

"Why are you suddenly trying to influence how people play?" I asked.

"Some book, I think," he shrugged. "Who knows? I just do as I'm told."

The book, of course, that has caused this new style of play to be seen more and more in American casinos is *Beat the Craps Out of the Casinos: How to Play Craps and Win.* In it I introduced you to the Captain, the greatest craps player in the world, and gave you the fundamentals of his Supersystem (sometimes called: *The 5-Count Doey-Don't).* I also introduced you to his Crew of 22 high rollers, some of whom I will discuss in this book also.

If you have not read *Beat the Craps Out of the Casinos: How to Play Craps and Win!*, I would strongly recommend that you do so before continuing with this book. Although each book can be read separately, I make certain assumptions in this book that I didn't make in *Beat the Craps Out of the Casinos;* the first is that you are fully aware of the percentages involved in all the bets on the layout, the second is that you are completely comfortable with the jargon of craps, the third is that you are fully aware of your own principles of money management. In short, *Beat the Craps Out of the Casinos* was the warm-up, this is the workout!

When *Beat the Craps Out of the Casinos: How to Play Craps and Win!* was first published in November of 1991 by Bonus Books of Chicago, I had no idea it would cause such controversy and recriminations on the part of casino personnel. Before its publication, there were five of us playing the Supersystem: the Captain, who originated it, two of his Crew, and me and my delightful partner A.P. As I related in *Beat the Craps Out of the Casinos*, occasionally A.P. and I would come in for some scorn when playing the Supersystem, because at first it does appear as if you don't know what you're doing. The scorn and anger were rarely for the fact that you were winning money. The pits didn't seem to notice or, at least, they didn't care or comment. One year later it's a whole different ball game. Now, thousands of people are playing the Supersystem, or, at the very least, incorporating the *5-Count* into their play.

The field of craps suckers has diminished, as has the casino's hold on these former fish. (Don't get me wrong: Supersystem-savvy players are still a tiny drop in the big bucket of otherwise bad players.) But that boxman at Binions was genuinely annoyed by the Supersystem and well he should be. He must realize that his casino's profits would plummet if everyone who played craps played this way.

The Supersystem does two things that irritate casinos: it tends to consistently lower your losses while simultaneously positioning you to take full advantage of good rolls. Sometimes the difference between a win and a loss for a session is how much you were losing before you started winning! The less you lose when you lose, the less you need to win to win overall! (That might sound like a Buddhist Koan but it does makes perfect sense!)

I find it flattering that the dealer at the Claridge had been told to help me select different bets. But when have any of you craps players seen dealers and pit bosses go out of their way to help players make "better" bets? Rarely. When some poor desert-drained, brain-dried schnook in Las Vegas plunks his hard earned prospecting money on the Big Six or the Big Eight, how many times do you see dealers recommend placing the six or eight on the board where he can at least get house odds on those numbers? When some drooling, besotted idiot slithers off the boardwalk in Atlantic City and staggers to a craps table and slobbers: "Give me a twelve, a yo and a barf bag," how many caring dealers try to explain to him that the house has a staggering edge on these bets? In fact, it's just the opposite as you know; the stickman's job is to hawk the very worst bets at a craps table - those proposition bets at the center that can suck the marrow from a gambler's bankroll faster than a vampire can suck the blood from a succulent young virgin. "Bet those hardways, go for the high-low, whirl anyone?" There is an almost constant stickman litany designed to lure you into doing something stupid. But now, suddenly, some casinos take the time to recommend playing in some other way instead of the Supersystem! Thanks for your care and concern fellas! But I'll pass.

So the fact that some casinos in both Vegas and Atlantic City are trying to discourage people from playing the Supersystem can only mean one thing - the casinos don't want players to play the Supersystem because it's costing the casinos money. That's logical. The Supersystem is doing what it is intended to do - decreasing losses due to horrendously cold rolls, while increasing profit potential during good rolls. Thus, the players are losing less and, I hope, winning more. This disconcerts the friends of friendly casinoland, whose sole joy rests in separating you from your money.

In addition, as many of you craps players know, the Supersystem has been outlawed from tournament play in most casinos sponsoring craps tournaments.

I can understand why.

Craps tournaments can be explosive and conservative play is often called for, especially early on. Indeed, *not losing* is often the same as *winning* in such games. I have no problem with tournaments outlawing the Supersystem for short term play. I also have no problem with casinos not wanting customers to have a viable method of holding down their losses and maximizing their wins. Casinos want and need stupid players and stupid play to keep their profits high. I understand and appreciate this. I just don't want to help them in this endeavor.

However, I do have a problem with surliness, nastiness, and stupidity. Sometimes these traits are in great abundance in a craps pit. Thankfully, at other times they are not.

I also know one thing the casinos don't know. I know how few people can actually put the Supersystem into play, not because they are intellectually incapable of doing so, but because they are emotionally unable to. Many otherwise intelligent people have told me why they can't play the Supersystem. Here are the most frequently cited reasons.

1. I don't want to wait for the *5-Count*. I can't stand staying at a table for long periods of time without placing a bet.

2. I want to get right into the action because I'm afraid of missing a good roll.

3. It's too slow.

4. The casinos won't comp me as they did before.

5. The other players look at me as if I'm nuts.

6. I get frustrated when a player makes his number right away and I'm not in the action.

7. I get frustrated when I've waited for the *5-Count* and then get blown out right off when I place my money at risk.

8. It's too difficult getting just the right spot at the table to do the Supersystem comfortably.

9. I don't like to ask the dealers to help me place some of the Don't Come bets because the dealers seem annoyed.

10. Too often I can't bet my favorite numbers.

11. You can't make that big killing with the Supersystem.

Actually, all of these are legitimate reasons for not playing the Captain's Supersystem.

The Captain: "I recognize that many people don't have the patience to play the Supersystem. Even waiting for the *5-Count* does take a measure of discipline. The Supersystem is not for the gambler who wants to make the big score once in his lifetime. It's for the player who wants to win in the long run. I don't make a killing playing as I do, I just win on a regular basis. A little here, a little there, it all adds up. Of course, the amount I win is in direct relation to the amount I bet and the amount of risk I'm willing to take. My wins might seem staggering to a small bettor but in reality they are only a small fraction of my total bets.

"It doesn't bother me that people don't want to play the Supersystem - for whatever reasons they give. Some of my closest Crew members just don't want to play it. It doesn't fit in with their aims for playing the game. Remember, not everyone gambles for the same reasons. For some, it's a thrill just walking up to a craps table, plunking their money down, making wild bets, screaming, hooting, cheering. They're playing for the fun of it. Winning or losing is just part of the fun. Others are desperately looking to score, looking for the hot roll that will bring them riches and an easy life. Still others just can't bring themselves to miss out on a few numbers which is necessary if you are going to play the Supersystem or use the 5-Count. They imagine that every single roll is the beginning of the BIG one. I tend to look at every single roll as merely a prelude to a seven. I'm always pleasantly surprised when a shooter has a good roll, and I'm never terribly disappointed when that seven appears. In fact, I prefer playing at ice cold tables where the 5-Count protects me perfectly than at lukewarm tables where I can get hurt if the shooters are hitting a few numbers and then sevening out. If you divide craps rolls into four types - cold, lukewarm, warm and hot - then three of them favor my Supersystem - cold, warm, and hot - and only one can hurt you - lukewarm. It is my opinion, based on playing craps for so many decades, that there are far more cold rolls than anything else and these cold rolls are what ultimately make most craps players losers. You've been blasted out so many times, and so quickly, with all your money up, that when a decent roll comes along you just can't break even for your craps career.

"The Supersystem is for serious craps players and by serious I mean craps players who want to play often and for years and grind out wins. Craps is a difficult game to beat. The house has built in a mathematical edge on every bet. You could never go to a casino every single day, bet every single roll of every single shooter - whether you're a right or a wrong bettor - and expect to win in the long run.

"I think of craps as a surfer thinks of a wave. You paddle out, that means you put your money on the table. Now, you want to catch the wave, a roll, that will bring you into shore. Most of the waves can't bring you home, they just aren't powerful enough. If you attempt to catch each wave that comes at you, shortly you will be exhausted, and when a wave sufficiently strong comes your way, you just won't have the energy to hop on it and ride it home. As a serious craps player you cannot bet every roll with every shooter. It's as simple as that. If you do, you will lose, period."

Of course, many craps players have realized this truism and have developed various methods for determining which shooters to bet on.

Some look for "the qualified shooter," that is, a shooter who has made his first point. The problem here is that a shooter can make dozens of numbers and never make a point, and an otherwise good roll will have been wasted. Some players say to "clock" the table, looking for the inside numbers to appear several times before going on them. That's interesting. But what if shooter "A" has been throwing inside numbers, does that mean shooter "B" will do so too? Of course not. Yet, both shooters "A" and "B" may have good rolls. By "clocking" a table, you'll miss the good shooters.

No system, be they in books or in ludicrously expensive seminars given by "highly successful" gamblers, has ever come up with a method for judging when to place your money at risk as has the Captain's *5-Count* and Supersystem.

My good friend Alan Tinker, an aficionado of craps and craps systems, gives an interesting explanation for the efficacy of the *5-Count* and the Supersystem.

Alan Tinker: "Really, what the *5-Count* is is the equivalent of going from table to table looking for a shooter who is having a decent roll and then jumping in. The difference of course is this: you aren't going from table to table looking for someone in the midst of a good roll. You are waiting for that roll by preserving your capital at a single table.

"The myth that you can walk around a casino and look for good rolls is just that - a myth. Anyone who has played craps in a casino knows that when a table is in the midst of a good roll, it is almost impossible to get into it. The table is usually packed. You're like a hyena trying to claw its way onto a kill. The 5-*Count* gives you a method for potentially being *already at the table, with most of your bankroll intact,* when the good roll begins. And by playing both sides of the board in the Supersystem, you aren't giving the house much of an edge when you win.

"I think one of the revolutionary ideas that the Captain articulates is so simple and self-evident, yet so few players fully grasp it: the casinos make their profits *when you win* by sharing your winnings with you! If that can get through to players then they will fully appreciate the Captain's methods of play. When the casino pays off its bets at less than true odds, as it does on every craps bet except the odds bets, then it has made itself your partner. The Supersystem, aside from its other inherent advantages, keeps this partnership to a minimum."

The Captain: "The Supersystem is not perfect. No method of play is. It's biggest disadvantage is the fact that people can and do seven out on the six, seven and eight counts. This can hurt you. But in these cases, you use money management to help you succeed. Never stay at a table where several shooters have sevened out immediately after the *5-Count.* Save your money. Walk away."

If you have been playing the Supersystem as outlined in *Beat the Craps Out of the Casinos,* or if you've incorporated the *5-Count* into your regular play, you know without question that there are more cold tables, with shooters sevening out within the *5-Count,* than there are lukewarm tables where shooters are sevening out on the sixth, seventh, and eighth rolls.

The book you're reading now is primarily geared to accomplishing five things for the serious player.

1. Give the player several ways of approaching the *Classic* Supersystem.

2. Define and analyze the *Radical* Supersystem which the Captain employs quite frequently.

3. Give a method for incorporating the Supersystem into a place betting strategy for the purpose of being comped.

4. Give the high roller or place bettor revolutionary new "buy" bets that will help cut the house edge.

5. Give the Captain an opportunity to answer directly the many questions that have been sent to me by readers of the first book, or asked me by players.

But first a little review.

Talk sense to a fool and he calls you foolish.

...Euripides

Chapter Two

The 5-Count Review

The *5-Count* is the foundation for all the Captain's strategies and must be understood and incorporated perfectly into whatever system(s) of play you eventually choose to utilize. The purpose of the *5-Count* is to avoid horrendous rolls of the dice, while simultaneously positioning yourself to take advantage of good rolls. How and why the *5-Count* works were fully explained in *Beat the Craps Out of the Casinos; How to Play Craps and Win!*

Nevertheless, here are the essentials. Learn them if you haven't already done so because the *5-Count* is the key that could unlock the casino treasure for you.

The *5-Count* always begins with a point number (four, five, six, eight, nine or 10) and ends with a point number.

The shooter is given the dice. He rolls a five. That's count number one or 1-Count. Had he rolled a two, three, seven, 11 or 12 on that first roll, there would be no count.

Rolls two, three and four can be any number, including a seven. (I'll explain this momentarily.) But roll five must be a point. If on the fifth roll, the shooter rolled a three, you would not have completed the *5-Count*. That three would not have counted at all.

Let's do it step by step.

Shooter rolls a seven on the come out.

No count.

Shooter rolls a three.

No count.

Shooter rolls a six.

1-Count.

Shooter rolls an eight.

2-Count.

Shooter rolls an 11.

3-Count

Shooter rolls a two.

4-Count.

Shooter rolls a three.

4-Count and holding.

Shooter rolls an 11.

4-Count and holding.

Shooter rolls a 10.

5-Count!

It is upon the completion of the *5-Count* that you will place money at risk.

There are times when the shooter makes his point before the *5-Count*. An example of such a roll follows; notice how the seven is treated in such a case.

Come out roll is six = 1-Count.

Shooter rolls a six, making his point = 2-Count.

Come out roll is a seven = 3-Count.

Come out roll is an 11 = 4-Count

Come out roll is a seven = 4-Count and holding.

Come out roll is a nine = *5-Count.*

Once again: *the 5-Count starts with a point number and ends with a point number.*

The Captain: "I think the *5-Count* is the single most important element in all my strategies because it automatically eliminates the rotten rolls. Now, some people who have incorporated the *5-Count* into their games will sometimes get upset that a shooter will make his point or a couple of numbers within the *5-Count,* and thus they aren't on them. Forget it. Just observe the game and you'll see that it is uncommon to find a table where shooter after shooter establishes a point, makes his point and then sevens out within the *5-Count.* More than likely, in fact inevitably, the rule for tables is that cold ones - those tables where the shooter sevens out immediately after establishing his point or within two or three rolls of it - are the *norm.*

"The *5-Count* also eliminates what I call *disinterested* shooters. You've seen these guys. They pretend not to care at all about their rolls. They take the dice, don't even look at the table, and just heave-ho! In my entire lifetime of playing craps, I have rarely seen these shooters have good rolls. The *disinterested* shooter is almost universally male. Almost every female I've encountered at a craps table takes some care with her roll."

Why is this important? Why shouldn't a shooter just fling the dice down the table without care? Isn't a craps roll just a random event? What possible good can come of caring about your roll?

The Captain: "I am a firm believer in *rhythmic rolling* which is the tendency for a shooter to get in a groove, to throw the dice mechanically the same way time and again. If the shooter is in a non-seven mode, you'll notice that more often than not he or she is fixing the dice a set way each time, and is throwing the dice precisely the same way roll after roll, and they are bouncing against the back wall the same way. More than likely numbers are bunching up. A string of nines, several tens in a row. Hardways of the same number back to back.

"Not everyone who has a good roll does this, I'll admit, but enough do that it is noticeable. So look for it the next time you play. And look for the casino personnel to try to disrupt the shooter's rhythm if the roll is getting costly to the casino. They'll bring out racks of new chips and place them in the center of the table. They'll start pushing the dice towards the shooter then quickly take them back as the shooter reaches for them. They'll examine the dice after every roll, as if the shooter has somehow switched his own into the game. They'll even glare at the shooter. I've seen more baleful looks on the part of boxmen and pit bosses than I have on professional boxers.

"If the shooter is a high-roller, the pit people will interrupt his rolling to ask for his name or they'll introduce themselves to him. All these activities, including verbally scolding the shooter to hit the back wall, are done to throw the shooter's rhythm off."

The Captain has a good point here. Recently, I was at Binions Horseshoe in Downtown Las Vegas and I was in the midst of a torrid roll. I like to fix my dice with the two threes in a "V" formation, but I do it so quickly now that the pit can't tell me to speed up. I fix them in one motion and throw. One of my dice went flying off the table. I had thrown it a little too high and it hit an area of the table with bounce, and off it went. The pit boss, who had been glaring at me in the hopes of breaking my rhythm, then interrupted the game. "Shooter you have to hit the back wall!" he said. The other players looked at him as if he were nuts. In the 15 minutes of my roll thus far I had not missed the back wall once. One of the other players said: "The dice went *off* the table for chrissakes! What back wall should he hit? The next table's?" Everyone laughed, the pit boss glared, and I rolled for another five minutes. But the pit is very conscious of what the Captain calls a shooter's rhythm. Many times I've seen a contented smirk on the part of some pit person when he feels he's broken a shooter's rhythm and that seven comes up.

The Captain: "Look also for a rhythmic shooter to become distracted by the arrival of his wife or girlfriend, or husband or boyfriend, or the cocktail waitress. Watch carefully as the rhythmic roller accidentally drops one die and then goes to shoot. He throws the dice differently and guess what? A seven! This is not superstition. This is observation of rhythmic rollers. You can observe this yourself. Notice how many times when a rhythmic roller's rhythm is broken that he or she rolls that damned seven. Just observe and I think you'll be surprised.

"Part of the reason I think the superstition that when the dice go off the table a seven will be thrown is that enough times in the collective consciousness of the craps playing public, a rhythmic roller lost his rhythm and threw the seven in such cases. It wasn't the dice going off the table that caused the seven, it was the roller's loss of rhythm that did it.

"By the way, I also think it is true that some people are lousy rollers. I have friends who have never, ever had a good roll, and they play frequently. What are the odds against someone who has played thousands of hours, rolled the dice thousands of times, never having a good roll? What are the odds against that? Staggering. I think many of these people are also *rhythmic rollers* in the worst way. They are *rhythmic seven shooters*. They are a Don't players dream, of course. But since I'm a right bettor, their negative rhythms don't do me any good.

"The *5-Count* eliminates the *disinterested* shooter in favor of the *rhythmic* non-seven mode shooter. The *disinterested* shooter almost seems happy when he sevens out, as if to say: 'Hey, I wasn't really trying.' The *rhythmic* one tends to get angry when he sevens out, as if it's his fault that the seven came up. I like that seriousness of purpose in a player. Who would you rather have rolling with your money on the line - the guy who expects to fail, or the guy who wants to win? If there is such a thing as psychokinesis, the ability to control material objects such as dice with the mind, then which of the two shooters would have a shot of doing this?

"As silly as it might seem at first, craps is not just a game of cold probabilities, and memory-less dice at all times with all shooters. Rather, it is a game of ebbs and flows, and rhythms and repetitions. And some shooters get in a non-seven mode, go with the flow, better than others. Most do it unconsciously, having hit upon a way of throwing for just this one turn at shooting; some having hit at a method of throwing that is the same every time out because it works for them. Over time the rhythmic roller has been conditioned by his successes, be it consciously or unconsciously, and thus fixes the dice a certain way, throws a certain way time and time again. I believe, based on my experience at the craps table, that you have a much better chance for a good roll from such a shooter, than from a disinterested one. The *5-Count* is geared to finding him.

"Most players aren't rolling rhythmically even when they get past the *5-Count*. So what? At their worst, non-rhythmic rollers are just playing that old-time craps of memory-less dice and cold fluctuations in probability. That's the way the casino likes it, too, because that's where the casino edge is. But even these shooters can have good rolls. The *5-Count* will protect you against their bad rolls, however."

Haste in every business brings failures.

...Herodotus

Chapter Three

The Classic Supersystem

In *Beat the Craps Out of the Casinos: How to Play Craps and Win!* I gave a general description of the Supersystem and how and why it works. I demonstrated a somewhat aggressive approach. Many readers wanted to know if that approach was the only or optimal way to play it.

The Captain: "There is no optimal way to play the Classic Supersystem, merely variations of preferment. If you have the bankroll and you like aggressive betting, then you'll play the Classic Supersystem aggressively. You do expose yourself to more risk playing aggressively but you simultaneously open yourself to more profit. If, however, you wish to conserve your bankroll, or are working with a small one, then obviously you will play more conservatively. How you play is up to you. But if you want to get the full benefits of the Supersystem, then there are two absolute laws you must follow: 1.) do not deviate from the *5-Count* procedure, and, 2.) take your bets off when the formula calls for it. Most people find this latter activity difficult. However, it is essential. If your numbers aren't hitting, in the long run you're better off out of the game.

"The common problem for many inveterate craps players who try the Supersystem is that they've waited an inordinate amount of time (for them) to get into the action, and now they're asked to get right back out. Do it."

The Conservative Classic Supersystem

In all Supersystem play, you will be placing bets on both sides of the board - Pass / Don't Pass, Come / Don't Come - at appropriate times during the *5-Count*. This method of betting is called the Doey-Don't. Some casino personnel have begun to call this approach "playing the odds." The house only has an edge on the initial placement of the Come portion of the bet and this only on the 12, which will come up an average of once every 36 rolls. However, once your initial bet is on the board, either on the Pass / Don't pass, or the Come / Don't Come, these bets are irrelevant because no money is at risk. If the seven should show, you lose on the "do" side, but you win on the "don't" side. If the player makes the number, then the reverse is true - you win on the "do" and lose on the "don't." You are looking to make your money on the "odds" bets where the casino has no edge whatsoever.

Of course, the fact that the casino has no edge on the odds bets does not mean the reverse, that you do have an edge. It simply means that it is a fair game.

If you can avoid the horrendous rolls, which is what the *5-Count* is intended to do, and not suffer the crippling of your bankroll, then you are in a position to take advantage of good rolls and not share a penny with the house as you win.

The Captain: "You are giving the casino a slight nibble at your bankroll on the 12 when you first place the Doey-Don't bet. That's the price of admission to the game. I don't like the straight Pass Line or straight Come bets because when you get on the number and it wins, the house becomes a big partner in the bet. On the four or 10, instead of getting two to one on the payoff, you get even money. That's the equivalent of the house *keeping* half your win.

"So I prefer to give them a little nibble on the 12 and keep the whole meal to myself on the other bets. Even the fact that you will win occasionally on the Pass Line and Come bets when the seven or 11 appears, does not make up for the forced partnership of those even money payoffs."

On the straight Pass Line and Come bets, for every $100 you would have won in a fair game, the house takes $7.41 out of your win as your partner. For Place bettors, it is a little better, though not significantly so. For every $100 in expected win, the house takes $6.25 as its share. But for the Doey-Don't player, the house takes a mere $1.39 for every $100 in expected wins. Now, these figures are for the standard double odds game found in most casinos.

For a 10 times odds game found in some Las Vegas casinos, the house would extract a staggeringly small 28 cents for every $100 in wins! It doesn't get much better than that. [For a fuller explanation of the superiority of the Doey-Don't over all other betting methods refer to *Beat the Craps Out of the Casinos: How to Play Craps and Win!* pages 49 - 54.]

Let us start with a new shooter.

His come out roll is a five. That is the 1-Count.

The next roll is a three = 2-Count.

His next roll is a six = 3-Count.

You now place a bet on the Come and a bet on the Don't Come.

His next roll is a four = 4-Count.

The dealer takes your Come and Don't Come bets and places them on the four.

You now place another Come and Don't Come bet.

The shooter's next roll is a six = 5-Count.

The dealer takes your Come and Don't Come bets and places them on the six. You now take the maximum odds on the Come portion of your two bets.

You now place another Come and Don't Come bet.

The shooter rolls an eight.

The dealer now places your Come and Don't Come bet on the eight.

You take the full odds on the Come portion of the bet.

You now have three numbers working for you, the four, six and eight. When one of these numbers hits, the dealer will pay off your odds bet at the true odds, give you even money for your Come bet, take your Don't Come bet, and then return both your original Come bet and your odds.

At this point, with only two numbers working, you will place another Come and Don't Come bet.

The Captain: "Having three numbers work for you is not an aggressive system but yet you do have enough action to capitalize on a good roll. However, with three numbers working, if none of your numbers hits within four rolls, you will call off your odds bets for two rolls. If the seven isn't rolled in those two rolls, you will tell the dealer that your odds are working again. Remember when calling off your bets, that you are calling off only the odds. Some sneaky pit people, irritated by your playing of the Supersystem, will sometimes instruct their dealers to 'take down' your Don't Come bets as well. Never allow this because you suddenly are at risk with your come bet. So be very clear that you are calling off only the *odds*.

"When your odds are off, it is possible that one or even two of your numbers will hit. If that happens simply place another Come and Don't Come bet immediately. Remember this, if one number hits when it's off, you wouldn't have made any money. With three bets, say the four, six, and eight of this example, you have to hit at least twice to have any chance of making a profit. If you did hit twice and then the shooter sevened out with you having two numbers working, you've made a slight profit. So don't get too upset if one of your off-numbers hits. If two numbers hit, then you've been slightly hurt. However, more often than not, the seven will come up in those two rolls, or two other numbers will hit instead of your numbers.

"You stay off for two rolls but you only call your bets on again if the second number is a point number - four, five, six, eight, nine or 10. Thus, on the second roll, if a three is thrown, you would not say that your odds are working again. Wait for a point number.

"In the Supersystem you are not looking for epic rolls of garbage numbers, so much as repetitions of the numbers you are on. It is far better to be on one number and have that hit four consecutive times before a seven, than to be on all the numbers and be dismayed as only a few of them hit among the twos, threes, elevens and twelves. If your numbers are not repeating, a shooter can be in a groove that doesn't help you. So take your odds off. Sometimes the difference between winning and losing is the one or two times you went off and the shooter rolled a seven."

When the shooter makes his point, you will place a Pass / Don't Pass bet if you are on two numbers. However, if you are on three numbers, then you have to decide if you want to take the extra risk and go up on a possible fourth number by betting the come out roll. When I'm playing conservatively, I do place a Pass / Don't Pass bet for two reasons: if the shooter rolls a seven on the come out, all my odds and my Don't Pass bet and win are returned to me. Now, I have no numbers working. The second reason I place a Pass / Don't Pass is to protect myself in case one of the numbers I'm already on becomes the point. I'll still be on three numbers as the shooter continues his roll.

The Aggressive Classic Supersystem

This variation of the Classic Supersystem has you working with four numbers.

Shooter rolls a five on come out roll = 1-Count.

Shooter rolls a six = 2-Count.

You now place a Come and Don't Come bet.

Shooter rolls an eight = 3-Count.

You now place a Come and Don't Come as the dealer places your bets on the eight.

Shooter rolls a 10 = 4-Count.

You now place a Come and Don't Come bet as the dealer places your previous bets on the 10.

Shooter rolls a six = 5-Count.

The dealer now places your Come and Don't Come bets on the six. You now give the dealer the correct odds for the Come bets on the three numbers eight, 10 and six.

You place another Come and Don't Come bet.

The shooter might roll a number you already have. You will continue to place Come and Don't Come bets until you have four numbers working. If you are never able to get up on four numbers that is more than likely due to the joyous fact that the shooter is rolling your numbers over and over, or, less likely and less joyous, he is rolling garbage numbers: two, three, 11, and 12.

When you are on *three* numbers in the aggressive Classic Supersystem, if the shooter should roll four times in a row without hitting any of your numbers, you call your odds off for two rolls. When you are up on *four* numbers, and the shooter rolls three times without hitting one of your numbers, you will call off your odds for two rolls. If the shooter doesn't seven out during those two rolls, you call your odds on again if the second roll is a point number, or until a point number is rolled. However, if the shooter once again doesn't hit your numbers for three rolls, you again will go off for two rolls. (This rarely happens.) And that is how you will continue until the shooter ultimately sevens out.

One more time: when you have three numbers working and the shooter doesn't roll one of them four consecutive times, call your odds off for two rolls. When you have four numbers working, call your odds off for two rolls if the shooter hasn't made one of them in three consecutive rolls. When your odds bets are off, the second roll must be a point number before you call your bets on again.

Keep in mind that if you are on the Pass / Don't Pass, you have to remove your odds yourself.

Thus: "I'm off on my odds."

Off roll is a two = 1-roll.

Off roll is a 12 = 1-roll and counting.

Off roll is a three = 1-roll and counting.

Off roll is a nine = 2-roll.

"My odds are working again!"

The shooter will now, hopefully, roll your numbers for the next five thousand consecutive rolls and you will never have to work another day in your life.

The holy passion of Friendship is of so sweet and steady and loyal and enduring a nature that it will last through a whole lifetime, if not asked to lend money.

...Mark Twain

Chapter Four

The Radical Supersystem

This next variation of the Supersystem is based upon the Captain's observation and belief that numbers tend to repeat, and that quite often and unexpectedly certain numbers will get hot, either due to the shooter's rhythmic roll, or due simply to random fluctuations in probability. The Captain plays the Radical Supersystem about 50 percent of the time, especially when the table is not too crowded.

Essentially, the Radical Supersystem is a follow-the-numbers approach and can be played either conservatively (three numbers working) or aggressively (four numbers working), depending on your predilection. Here's how it works.

The shooter comes out with a five = 1-Count.

Place a Come and a Don't Come bet.

The shooter rolls a six = 2-Count.

Place a Come and a Don't Come bet.

The shooter rolls a nine = 3-Count.

Place a Come and a Don't Come bet.

The shooter rolls a 10 = 4-Count.

Place a Come and Don't Come bet.

The shooter rolls an eight = 5-Count.

If you wish to have only three numbers working, you will tell the dealer to place odds on the *last three numbers rolled*, in this case the nine, 10, and eight. Say: "Odds on nine, 10 and eight."

You again place a Come and Don't Come bet.

The shooter rolls a six.

Since you have a Come and Don't Come bet already on the six, without odds on the Come, the dealer will pay your Come portion and take your Don't Come portion. You will immediately do the following:

1.) replace the Don't Come bet

2.) tell the dealer to give you the odds on the six

3.) tell the dealer to take your odds down from the nine.

You will now be on the 10, eight, and six which were the last three numbers to hit.

You will always be placing Come and Don't Come bets in the Radical Supersystem but you keep having the odds on the last three numbers that hit (or the last four if you wish to play aggressively).

The Captain: "The Radical Supersystem is my favorite way to play and I have had greater success with it than any other way of playing. However, there are times when it is not feasible to play it. If you're at a crowded table, and the dealers are harried, you'll be slowing down the action by constantly asking for your bets to be moved.

"Also, if you are in the midst of a good roll, you don't want the shooter to become distracted, especially if he's been rhythmically rolling. In addition, once the dealer becomes rattled, he stands a good chance of messing up your bets and payoffs, and before you know it the pit boss is involved and the game has come to a halt. But more often than not, table conditions are not such that you won't be able to play it.

"The Radical Supersystem calls for you to be on the ball, too. You have to keep track of the last numbers that have hit and in what order. You have to be clear in your directions to the dealers. The benefits of playing this way are self-evident. If a shooter should throw a series of the same number, you will be on that number at all times. You won't be on, then off, then on, then off, as you would be in the Classic Supersystem of three numbers working.

"You will, however, follow certain off procedures as before. If you are working with three numbers and the shooter rolls four garbage numbers - two, three, 11, or 12 - then you will continue to make Come and Don't Come bets, but you will call off the odds for two rolls. Thus, you will still be on the numbers when you call your bets working. If you have been working with four numbers, then you will call off your bets if three garbage numbers are rolled."

The only real change in procedure is the fact that you will not call your bets off if you are following numbers around the board without hitting. For example, if you have the six, eight and nine working (they were rolled in that order) and the next four rolls consist of 10, five, six, and four, you haven't made a nickel, and four rolls have gone by (you were originally on the six but you moved your odds to the 10). The shooter is rolling numbers, you just haven't been lucky enough to be on those numbers. Although you are obviously taking a risk, you will stick with the shooter and the Radical Supersystem in such a case, or you will revert to the Classic Supersystem.

The Captain: "As in any system of play, there is a downside to the Radical Supersystem. Although it is rare, the above scenario can happen as you follow the numbers. There are no immediate repetitions of the three or four numbers you have working and as you take the odds from the oldest number to put them on the new number, the old one hits. There are certain nightmare scenarios in Supersystem play and that's one of them. Now, if you find that this is happening, immediately switch to the Classic Supersystem, and stay on the numbers you have. Hopefully, one or more of them will hit within the specified number of rolls.

"You can't be an automaton at the craps table as you play the variations of the Supersystem. You must be flexible and ready to switch back and forth. In a sense, you are trying to position yourself to take advantage of the flow, be it random and choppy, random and repetitious, or rhythmic and reliable."

Let's take a look at a series of rolls and apply the Radical Supersystem to it.

Shooter / Number Count / *Situation*	Numbers/**Odds working in bold**
Shooter comes out with a seven = 0-Count.	-------
Shooter comes out with a nine = 1-Count.	-------
Shooter's point is a nine.	
Shooter rolls a three = 2-Count.	-------
Place a Come and Don't Come bet.	
Shooter rolls a six = 3-Count.	6
Place a Come and Don't Come bet.	
Shooter rolls a five = 4-Count.	6, 5
Place a Come and Don't Come bet.	
Shooter rolls an eight = 5-Count.	**6, 5, 8**
Place a Come and Don't Come bet.	
Shooter rolls a four.	6, **5, 8, 4**
Place a Come and Don't Come bet.	
Shooter rolls a 10.	6, 5, **8, 4, 10**
Place a Come and Don't Come bet.	
Shooter rolls an eight.	6, 5, **4, 10, 8**
Place a Come and Don't Come bet.	
Shooter rolls a 10.	6, 5, **4, 8, 10**
Place a Come and Don't Come bet.	
Shooter rolls a nine, making his point.	6, 5, 4, **8, 10, 9**

Place a Pass and Don't Pass bet.

(Your numbers will not be working on a come out roll)

Shooter comes out with a six.   5, 4, 8, **10, 9, 6**

Place a Come and Don't Come bet.

Shooter rolls a 10.   5, 4, 8, **9, 6, 10**

Place a Come and Don't Come bet.

Shooter rolls a six, making his point.   5, 4, 8, **9, 10, 6**

Place a Pass and Don't Pass bet.

(Your numbers will not be working on a come out roll.)

Shooter comes out with an 11.

Shooter comes out with a seven.

The dealer will now return all your odds, take your Come bets, and pay off and return your Don't Come bets. He will pay off your Pass Line bet and take your Don't Pass bet. Place another Don't Pass bet.)

Shooter comes out with an eight.   **8**

Place a Come and Don't Come bet.

Shooter rolls a six.   **8, 6**

Place a Come and Don't Come bet.

Shooter rolls a four.   **8, 6, 4**

Place a Come and Don't Come bet.

Shooter rolls a three.   **8, 6, 4**

Replace your Come bet, take your Don't Come win.

Shooter rolls a two.   **8, 6, 4**

Replace your Come bet, take your Don't Come win.

Shooter rolls an eleven.   **8, 6, 4**

Replace your Don't Come bet, take your Come win.

Shooter rolls a twelve.   8, 6, 4

Replace your Come bet. Call off the odds.

Place a Come and Don't Come bet.

Shooter rolls a nine.   8, 6, 4, 9

Place a Come and Don't Come bet.

Shooter rolls a five.   8, 6, **4, 9, 5**

Tell the dealer that your odds are to be moved from the six to the five, take your odds off the Pass Line bet of eight, and tell the dealer to place the odds on the nine. Your odds are now working.

Place a Come and Don't Come bet.

Shooter rolls a five.   8, 6, **4, 9, 5**

Place a Come and Don't Come bet.

Shooter rolls a nine.   8, 6, **4, 5, 9**

Place a Come and Don't Come bet.

Shooter rolls a five.   8, 6, **4, 9, 5**

Place a Come and Don't Come bet.

Shooter rolls a nine.   8, 6, **4, 5, 9**

Place a Come and Don't Come bet.

Shooter rolls a seven.   ~~8, 6, **4, 5, 9**~~

The dealer will take your Come bets and your odds, he will pay off and return your Don't Come bets.

The above series was taken from an actual game I played at Binions Horseshoe in the summer of 1992. You will note that during the last series the numbers five and nine were hit in repeating or alternating sequences. This is the desired result from the Radical Supersystem, repeating numbers that you are on. This sequence also had a 12 appear, the only edge the casino has on you, as well as a seven on the come out that resulted in the odds being returned along with the Don't Come bets and their payoffs. In a case such as this, you simply begin from scratch with your Pass and Don't Pass bets.

Sometimes the shooter will seven out immediately after establishing another point and you're thankful that your odds were returned since you only lost on one number, the Pass Line bet, as opposed to three or four numbers.

Fortune is like the market, where many times, if you can stay a little, the price will fall.

...Sir Francis Bacon

## Chapter Five

Comps, Pit Crews, Ratings and The Supersystem

For those of you who have played the Supersystem and then tried to get comped, you know the reaction of the pit crew to you. First they look at you like you're crazy, then they politely turn you down by claiming: "Sorry, sir, you aren't giving us enough action." You and I both know what the statement "action" means in this context. You aren't giving the casino enough of an edge on your bets to make even the most simple of complimentaries worth the casino's while.

Is there a way for a high roller to incorporate the Supersystem into his play and still be accorded full comp privileges?

The Captain: "You cannot play the Supersystem or one of its variations and expect to get fully comped unless you're betting a minimum of perhaps $50 on the Do and the Don't. The casino will figure, correctly, that they have that one in 36 edge on the 12 and that will probably satisfy them.

"Then again some of the bigger casinos, catering to the super-high-roller crowd, might even find this too paltry to consider for full comp privileges.

"I have never been an advocate of playing to impress the pit in order to get comped. I am an advocate of attempting to fool the pit into giving comps commensurate with a greater level of risk than you are actually taking. The *5-Count* was originally intended to stretch my physical time at the table but not my "risk" time. It wasn't until I had played it for an extended period that I realized how much it protected me against disastrous rolls. I was winning more because I was losing less, and I was still being fully comped.

"If you are not interested in getting comps then play the variations of the Supersystem as already given. However, if being comped appeals to you then there is a way to incorporate the Supersystem into your play."

Getting Rated

Casinos rate players based upon the following criteria:

1.) the edge the casino has on your type of betting.

2.) the number and amount of your bets in relation to the casino edge.

3.) the number of hours you spend at the table.

4.) the amount of money you're willing to lose based

on your history of play.

Let us take each of these areas separately.

The Casino's Edge

The casinos do not factor in the odds bets generally because the odds bets are considered a break even proposition for both the player and the casino. Casinos prefer players who bet the proposition bets such as the hardways, any craps and the like. These bets carry a heavy tax for the casino as you know. So a player who bets the 12 on every roll for $25 will get a better rating than someone placing the six for $30 because he stands to lose more in the long run.

As a general rule casinos prefer proposition bets to place bets and both of these to Pass and Come bets and all of them to the Supersystem.

The Captain: "You can consider the rating of bets as a *Stupidity Quotient*. The stupider your bets, the more highly you are prized by the casino, and the more comps you will get. The more idiotic you are at a gaming table, the more you are treated with respect. The casino world is the reverse of our culture, where intelligence and perception are highly prized. Instead, in the world of the casino they want dimwits to go along with their dim lights. Remember that the casino never really gives anything away for free. Those comps are usually paid for tenfold."

The Number and the Amount of Your Bets

The casinos prefer players who bet big and bet wide. A player who spreads out across the board, betting yos and hardways, placing the four and 10, betting the field and any seven, is highly rated compared to one who bets the Pass Line and takes the odds and then places a Come bet and takes the odds when he goes up on the number. The casino will make more money in the long run from the wildman than from the controlled player and thus the wildman is afforded more of the privileges of civilization: gourmet meals, the finest rooms, the best seats at shows and fights.

Obviously, the higher a person bets is also taken into consideration. Indeed, it is a key variable. If our wildman is betting a dollar on each of his proposition bets and place bets, and our controlled player is betting a hundred dollars on the Pass Line and Come, then the casino will rate the controlled player more highly since a smaller percentage of a big bet makes more money for the casino than a larger percentage of a small bet. But all things being equal, the greater the number and variety of bets, the better the rating.

The Amount of Playing Time

In general, the smaller the edge the casino has on you, the longer it will take for your bankroll to be ground down. Thus, the casino wants you to play as long as you possibly can so that their edge will win out. Usually, four hours a day is what a casino expects in action for full comp privileges. Four hours of playing craps is a long time, even if you break up your playing into four sessions of an hour each. In a four-hour period you can be assured that there will be a stretch where the seven comes up so frequently one or two rolls after the shooter establishes his point that you will have to pinch yourself to make sure you are in reality and not a nightmare. Somewhere in that four-hour span the casino will take the heart out of enough bankrolls that it will gladly give its big players all the comped amenities they desire.

The Captain: "In craps, time is on the side of the casino. The game is structured to whittle away at the smart player and hack away at the idiot. The mathematics of craps are indisputable. The casino does have an edge on every bet except the odds bets. To have any hope of whittling away at the casino, you have to develop a system of betting that strips the casino's edge to its minimum and lets you take maximum advantage of good rolls and fair payoffs.

"However, if you want to get comped, you have to do the opposite. You must bet poorly and often enough to make the casino's edge take effect. The dilemma we face in trying to get comped without incurring the full risk is this: how to *appear* stupid but *play* smart."

What Are You Willing to Lose?

Casinos want repeat customers, especially if these customers are not afraid of losing and losing big. They would rather have you lose $10,000 in one hour, than $400 in four hours. The bottom line to the casino is how much money you're willing to let them take from you. This is why the big baccarat players are at such a premium. Baccarat has a very low house percentage, as you know. Yet, a baccarat pit in a major casino can gross that casino millions because of the high-stakes players involved. When the casino analyzes your action it will decide whether you are the type of player who is willing to lose enough to make it worth their efforts to wine and dine you.

If you come to the table and bet $100 on the Pass Line and the shooter rolls 50 sevens and elevens in a row, then he establishes his point and makes his point, then he rolls for 10 straight days as you keep betting a hundred on the Pass Line and the Come and backing every single bet with full odds, the casino does not know if you are really a big player or not.

Your initial bet would indicate that you are but who really knows?

It's common knowledge that people will tend to escalate their bets during hot rolls so that by the time a shooter sevens out a $10 bettor is suddenly a $100 bettor. I saw just such a thing happen at the Frontier in Las Vegas in April of 1992. Two shooters, one after another, had torrid rolls of approximately 40 minutes each. The table had a dollar minimum bet with 10 times odds allowed. Half the table bet the minimum on the Pass Line and the Come at the beginning of the first shooter's roll. By the end of the second shooter's roll, no one was betting less than $10 on the Pass Line and backing it with $100 in odds! Some people were up to $25 and $250. The Place bettors who had started with $6 sixes and eights were hitting triple digits on all the numbers. Everyone looked like a high roller during that span of time. But were they? Of course not. Nor did the casino rate these players as such.

So our original player who plunks his $100 on the Pass Line appears to be a high roller but is he? How can the casino be sure? The casino hopes he will play a few times so the pit can get a chance to judge and accurately rate what kind of player he is. On his second visit, say, he loses his first two Pass Line bets and quits. He doesn't play again. On his next visit, he does the same thing. Is he a high roller or just someone with a few hundred dollars going all in right away?

Obviously, he is the latter.

Now, the reverse is also true. Let us take the individual who bets $25 on the Pass Line and tries to always have two Come bets working during a roll. At first he appears to be a medium roller and a very controlled player to a big casino. But after a few visits, the casino realizes that this guy plays 10 hours a day at this rate and is willing to lose $10,000, which he has done on several occasions. He will be quickly rated one of their top customers.

The Captain: "The casino's formula goes something like this: casino's average edge on all your bets combined, multiplied by the average amount of money you bet, multiplied by the number of hours you play (plus or minus what you are willing to lose) equals what you are worth to them.

"Now, the player who wishes to be comped but doesn't want to be taken, has to create his own formula. Are the comps worth the risk you're taking? This is the formula I use to decide whether to play for a comp at a hotel. Say I wish to see Sinatra on a weekend in Atlantic City, how much would the tickets cost me? Two hundred dollars per ticket. So that would be $400 for my wife and me. Now, I want a comfortable table, preferably a booth just for my party of four. How much of a bribe would I have to give the maitre d'? Probably $50 because the comped players would have had these tables reserved by the casino's hosts.

"So, just to see Frank Sinatra, we're talking $450. How much for a bottle of good wine at our table? Seventy-five dollars probably. Now, we're up to $525 just for the show portion of the weekend.

"Now, let's consider the room. The average price of the average room in a hotel in Atlantic City is about $165 a night. I'm not talking about a suite, just an average room. Of course, in Atlantic City you can't get a room on a Saturday night if you aren't somewhat of a big player, but we'll forget that for now. Let us say I'm staying Friday night and Saturday night. That's $330 just for the room. Now, you have meals. My wife and I are simple eaters and when we arrive on Friday afternoon, we'll have a light lunch that will cost no more than $20. For dinner on Friday night, however, we'll go gourmet. We're looking at a check of approximately $120. I won't count tips because you have to tip even when you're comped. So Friday's food bill is $140.

"Now, it's Saturday. A light breakfast for two? How does $16 sound? Now, lunch. Another $20. Now, a good dinner. Another $120. So Saturday's food bill comes to $156. Now, my wife likes to do a little shopping in the hotel gift shop. Nothing big. She averages about $40 a visit.

"Of course, you have breakfast on Sunday morning, another $16, then lunch, $20, then we go home. Should we factor in transportation? I think so. For me, the round trip from my home to Atlantic City takes a half tank of gas and $6 in tolls. Let's say transportation is $10. Now let's add it up.

Frank Sinatra	$525
Hotel Room	$330
Friday Food	$140
Saturday Food	$156
Sunday Food	$36
Shopping	$40
Transportation	$10
	———
Grand Total	$1,237

"So it would cost me $1,237 dollars if I wanted to see Frank Sinatra in Atlantic City on a given weekend. Of course, it would be considerably less for a lesser name. So for a smaller show or a lesser name, knock off about $300 from the entertainment expense. Then you're talking about a $937 bill. Of course, you can go the opposite way and say: 'I'll take a limo to Atlantic City and stay in a suite.' Since high rollers are often taken by limo (I call them *sheep-to-the-slaughter-mobiles*) and stay in suites, you would increase your expenses quite a bit.

"But let's keep our example of the Sinatra weekend, because high rollers love to be comped to Sinatra, but we'll stay in an average room and use our own transportation. If the casino is giving you this weekend for free, they are giving you a value of approximately $1,237. They expect to get that value back twice over when you lose at the tables.

"The way I look at it, I am starting with a *win* of $1,237! My problem is how not to lose that win either at the tables in actual money or because the casino won't rate me highly enough to comp me the weekend.

"My formula is simple. It's the same as the casino's except for a single word added to the equation. The *perceived* average edge of all your bets combined, multiplied by the *perceived* average amount of money you're betting, multiplied by the *perceived* number of hours you play (plus or minus what you are *perceived* as willing to lose) equals what they *perceive* you are worth to them.

"That word - perception - holds the key for the astute high roller. Does any intelligent human being, without a gambling problem, really want to lose bundles of money in a casino? I think not. Yet, intelligent people enjoy the fuss the casino hosts make over them when they are perceived as high rollers. It's fun to be treated like a king, no doubt about it. But it's even more fun to be treated like a king and not have to pay a king's ransom for the honor!

"So how can I be perceived as betting enough with enough of a casino edge for long enough to get what I want and not give them what they want? The *5-Count* gives you the body time at the table without the financial risk. All the rolls that you are not betting reduces the inexorable grinding down of your bankroll. With the *5-Count* the casino will give you a four-hour rating if your body is at the table that long, even if your money isn't at risk for the entire period of time.

"Now during the 5-Count you will not place any Doey-Don't bets because the person rating you looks a your initial bet to get a handle on you. So, your initial bet has to fit the profile of a high roller. On the 5-Count place $180 on the table and as loudly as you can without screaming say: "Ninety dollars on the six and eight!" Make sure the pit crew hears the bet.

"You are not going to leave these bets up for long on any given shooter, unless of course the shooter is hitting them. Now, with absolutely no fanfare whatsoever, you place a Come and Don't Come bet whose odds would approximately equal $90. If you are at a double odds table, then put $35 on the Come and Don't Come. When your number goes up, if it is a four or 10, you'll back it with $70 in odds; if it's a five or nine, you'll back it with $80 in odds; if it's the six or eight you'll tell the dealer loudly: 'Give me a $100 in odds on the six!" and more quietly: "Return the rest of my place bet." Thus, when a Doey-Don't goes up on the six or eight, you will be withdrawing the place bet and taking the odds. However, once you have three Doey-Don't bets working, even if they are not replacements for the six and eight, you will take down your place bets. Essentially, you will be playing the Supersystem on all but the initial bets after the 5-Count."

Let's go through it step by step.
Shooter rolls a five on the come out = 1-Count.

You do not place any bets.

Shooter rolls a six = 2-Count.

You do not place any bets.

Shooter rolls a nine = 3-Count.

You do not place any bets.

Shooter rolls an eleven = 4-Count.

You do not place any bets.

Shooter rolls a three = 4-Count and holding.

You do not place any bets.

Shooter rolls an eight = 5-Count.

You tell the dealer loudly: "Give me $90 on the six and the eight!"

You now place a Come and Don't Come bet.

Shooter rolls a 10.

You take full odds behind the Come bet. You place another Come and Don't Come bet.

Shooter rolls a six.

You tell the dealer to give you the full odds on the Come portion of the six and return the rest of your Place bet.

You place a Come and Don't Come bet.

Shooter rolls a four.

You tell the dealer to give you full odds on the four and to take down your eight.

You now have three numbers working if you are a conservative player. If you wished to have four numbers working, you would leave the eight up until it is replaced by a

Come / Don't Come bet, or until a fourth Come and Don't Come number was established.

The Captain: " Should the shooter make his point on the 4-Count, meaning his next roll will be a come out roll, then you would loudly say: "Place the six and eight for $90!" You're getting in the game earlier, but you're not at risk. The pit writes down your bet but since it's the come out roll, the bet is off. Don't even bother placing a Pass Line and Don't Pass bet. If the shooter throws a number of sevens, elevens, twos, threes, twelves, time is passing, you're being rated on your two place bets but you're not at risk! That's the best of all possible worlds, being rated when you're not at risk.

"You will find that by using the *5-Count* in this manner and then switching over to the Supersystem after the initial place bets of six and eight, you aren't giving the casino all that much of an edge on your bets, yet you should get the full array of comps. Some casinos might want an initial bet of $120 on the six and eight for the full array of comps. For a Sinatra weekend, this would not be an outrageous amount to bet. Remember: the *5-Count* gives you body time at a table without risk, placing the six and eight on a 4-Count during the come out gives you more *perceived* risk time on a place bet, and substituting the Supersystem gradually for the place bets will allow you to take advantage of repeating numbers without the casino sharing in your wins. The idea is to win a little and get the $1,237 in comps!

"Will this system *always* work? Of course not. But it will work a lot better and lot more often than the average high roller's betting method. The average high roller will lose a lot more than $1,237 on a given weekend. He'll lose more like $3,000 to $20,000! If you can just keep your losses under what the casino is giving you in value, then in reality you are a winner!

"However, you don't really want to *appear* to be a winner. So if you find that you are accumulating chips, hide a few of the $25 ones. Don't grab a handful of hundred and five-hundred dollar chips because the pit personnel eye these constantly. Siphon off the $25 chips. If you have a big win and you're coloring up at the table, place some chips in your pocket as you're fumbling to put the piles on the layout. Never let the casino know how much you've won. Even if you've lost, still hide some remaining chips. If you've lost $100, try to make it look as if you lost $300. If the table is crowded, don't even bother coloring up. Just go to the casino cage. But at all times, show the pit crews that you're willing to be a good and a big loser."

By using the methods described above, you can get your comps and your victory, too.

Getting along with women,
Knocking around with men,
Having more credit than money,
Thus one goes through the world.

...Johann W. von Goethe

## Chapter Six

The Best "Buys" at Craps and High-Rolling Without the High Risk

Craps is a game that offers the player a cornucopia of betting opportunities and decisions. It's a veritable flea market of bets and like most markets it's "buyer beware!" because not all bets return good value for your investment. The reason for this is simple: most bets in craps give the casino an enormous mathematical edge, one that is too difficult to overcome in the long run.

The Captain developed his Supersystem to cut this edge to its lowest by waiting for the *5-Count* and betting the Doey-Don't.

The Captain: "As I've stated in *Beat the Craps Out of the Casinos*, I look at craps as a series of fluctuations in probability punctuated by moments of rhythmic rolling where a shooter gets into a non-seven or repeating numbers mode. As a series, when you observe craps rolls, you notice that there are short bursts, where the shooter sevens out within five rolls, interrupted on occasion by longer rolls, "hot" rolls, with here and there the lukewarm rolls which are disadvantageous to the Supersystem player.

"With patience and proper application of the Classic or Radical Supersystem, I believe a player stands a great chance of winning in the long run. However, I recognize that many players are not really interested in the long run since they are only occasional players. Still, to these I would recommend the variations of the Supersystem. Yet, I know full well that not everyone can or wants to play it.

"If you are a high roller who enjoys place betting, you probably want to plunk your money down and root and cheer. That's fine. Everyone gambles for his own reasons, and as long as you can afford the thrill, I say - enjoy yourself! But if you want to be a high roller and/or a place bettor, why not try to get the best buy for your buck?"

Most high rollers tend to be place/buy bettors because they like the action of being able to go directly on the numbers and not have to wait on the Come for a number to be made, and then again for that same number to hit a second time before getting a payoff. Generally, the only gambling mathematics they're interested in is the speed with which they can get those bets onto the layout. Placing the numbers is a speedy way to get deep into the action.

The place bettor faces a manageable casino edge of 1.5 percent, sometimes call vigorish or vig, when the number being placed is either a six or an eight. This is not a bad bet if placing the numbers is your style. Unfortunately, the casino's edge in placing the five and nine, and the four and 10 is quite steep, 4 percent and 6.7 percent respectively.

Now, what does that mean for the place bettor? Let's chuck the language of percentages and talk money. After all, most of us live in our pockets and not our pocket calculators.

When you place the five or the nine for $10, you win $14. While this might sound good, the fact is you should have won $15! That's because the true odds on making either the five or the nine are three to two. There are six ways of making that abominable seven and four ways of making a five or nine. Essentially the casino "taxed" you one dollar for the privilege of placing the number. The casino became your partner when you won. Of course, when you lose you can't take back a dollar as your share of the casino partnership. When you lose, you're a sole proprietor.

On the four and 10 it's even worse. Place either one for $10 and a win pays $18. Not too shabby? It's worse than shabby; it's shameful. The four or 10 should be paid off at true odds of two to one (six ways to make the seven as opposed to three ways of making a four or a 10). Thus, the casino should have paid you $20 but instead it metaphorically reached across the table and snatched the two dollars from you as its share in your winnings.

Are there ways of placing the five and nine, four and 10, without having to share so much with the casino?

Yes.

Traditionally, place bettors have "bought" the four or 10 by paying a dollar tax ahead of time when placing these numbers for $20. The casinos then paid off the bet at the correct odds of two to one. Some savvy gamblers then "pushed the house" into accepting $25 buy bets for a dollar, thus reducing the house edge to 3.8 percent on the four and 10.

This was pretty much the standard until the Captain "pushed the house" for an even higher buy of the four and 10. Now, you could pay that dollar tax in advance and get true odds on a bet of $35. I wrote about the original "pushing" of Atlantic City in *Beat the Craps Out of the Casinos*.

Now, the Captain has come up with two new and revolutionary buy bets in the years since my researching and writing of *Beat the Craps Out of the Casinos*. One of them involves buying the five and nine, until now a usually idiotic move.

Before I explain the bets, let me preface by saying that not everyone is in a position to take advantage of the Captain's latest "pushing" of the casinos. These bets are more in keeping with the bankroll of a high roller and cannot be found on the lower betting denominations.

Of course, the term "pushing the casino" means getting a better game than advertised. Here the player attempts a bet that gives him a better edge, or, more accurately, takes away part of the built-in casino edge.

Not every casino will accept the following buy bets. Most Atlantic City casinos will, as will some Vegas casinos. But don't hesitate to make them. Some dealers will reject them out of hand. If they do, ask to see a pit boss. You'd be surprised how many casinos will go along with radically new bets - as these two are. Just give them a try.

First let's take the traditional buy of the four or 10.

In most casinos, you'll see craps players buying these for $25. Those who have read *Beat the Craps Out of the Casinos* or who have been influenced by the Captain's previous pushing of Atlantic City, can be found buying these numbers for $35 for the same one dollar tax. Here's the new push: instead of buying these numbers for $35, buy them for $39. You'll still only pay that one dollar tax but now you're getting an extra four dollars on the table at true odds.

How good is this bet when compared to the traditional place bet? Quite good.

Had you placed the four or 10 for $40, you would have won $72 when the number was made. Buying it for $39 gives you a win of $78. That's a substantial difference of six dollars. (Remember, you are actually putting up $40 on this bet because you must give the casino a dollar in taxes beforehand.) In the course of an extended period of play those six dollar differentials can amount to quite a bit of money. So, if you can afford to bet $40 on a number, buy the four or 10 for $39.

The next bet is truly revolutionary for a buy. Place $39 on the table and say: "Buy the five (or nine) for $38!" The casino will take the dollar advance tax out and then pay you the true odds of three to two on your five or nine.

Normally, it would be stupid to buy the five or nine. Why pay a tax in advance which is higher than the tax taken out after a win? But at the $38 mark, the reverse is true. The buy becomes a better bet. This is easily demonstrated.

You put up $39 to buy the five or nine for $38. The casino takes its one dollar tax. You win on the number and the casino pays you $57. Had you simply placed the five or nine for $40, you would have won $56. Thus, the traditional five and nine place bettor risks a dollar more to win a dollar less, while our revolutionary buy bettor risks a dollar less to win a dollar more.

You might ask: "What's a dollar more or less?"

To me a dollar means something. Those dollars saved by betting less but earning more can add up over the long haul into a hefty savings. Sometimes they can mean the difference between a winning or losing session.

As I've stated, not all casinos will take these bets. Indeed, except where the Captain and I have placed them, most casinos have never encountered them before.

The first time I ever bought the nine for $38 was at Tropworld in Atlantic City. When I placed my money on the table and said: "Buy the nine for $38," the dealers looked at me as if I were nuts.

"What?" asked one of them.

"I want to buy the nine for $38," I repeated.

One helpful, crusty, old craps player said: "That's a stupid bet, just place it for $40." I ignored him.

The dealer took my money but called over the pit boss. When the pit boss was informed that I wanted to buy the nine, he went into peals of derisive laughter. He looked at me and shook his head. Obviously, he knew something about the game and had been conditioned to believe that you never buy the five or nine.

"Sure, sure," he guffawed. "Would you like to buy the five, too? We're having a sale! Ha! Ha! Ha! How much did you want to buy it for?"

The dealer told him: "Thirty-eight dollars."

The pit boss paused and looked at me strangely. He nodded to the dealer. They had bought my buy, so to speak.

The pit boss then grabbed a piece of paper and a pen and did a little figuring. As the gods of craps would have it, the shooter rolled that nine. As I was being paid off, the pit boss came over to me and said politely: "That dollar means an awful lot to you doesn't it?"

I answered him politely: "Actually it's two dollars, one less on the bet, one more on the payoff. They mean a lot more to me than they do to Tropworld."

So there they are, the two very best buys at craps, if you can afford to make them. Neither of them has ever been written about before.

Although place betting is not the most efficient way to take your whacks at the casino bankroll (the Supersystem is) if you are the type who must place the numbers, then by all means buy into these buys. They'll make you a better place bettor.

The Captain: "In placing or buying the numbers, I would still recommend using the *5-Count*. In fact, one way to do your place and buy betting is to follow the numbers as the *5-Count* is progressing and bet them when the count is completed."

Place, Buy, and Following the Numbers

Here are two methods of placing and buying the numbers. In method one is you place/buy three or four numbers based upon the *5-Count* and then stay on them the appropriate number of rolls. The procedure is the same as in the Supersystem, except you're placing and buying the numbers.

Method One

Shooter comes out with a six = 1-Count.
Shooter rolls a five = 2-Count.
Shooter rolls a three = 3-Count.
Shooter rolls a 10 = 4-Count.

Shooter rolls a nine = 5-Count.

Tell the dealer to buy the five and nine for $38 each and to buy the 10 for $39.

If you wish to work with four numbers, simply place or buy whatever number is rolled next. Now, you wait and hope these numbers hit. If you are up on three numbers, you will call off your bets if none of your numbers hits in four rolls. If you are on four numbers, you will call off your bets if none of your numbers hits after three rolls. In each case, you will stay off for two rolls and go back on if the second roll is a point number or whenever the first point number hits after the second roll.

Method Two

Shooter comes out with a six = 1-Count.
Shooter rolls an eight = 2-Count.
Shooter rolls a five = 3-Count.
Shooter rolls a nine = 4-Count.
Shooter rolls a 10 = 5-Count.
Buy the five and nine for $38 each and the 10 for $39.
Shooter rolls an eight.

If you wish to work with four numbers, place the eight for $60. If you wish to work with only three numbers, remove the earliest number hit, in this case the five, and bet the eight. You will always follow the numbers by betting the last number to hit and taking down the earliest number.

This method of betting is the exact same as the Radical Supersystem in that you are following the numbers, looking for a series of hits or "hot" numbers. Where it differs, of course, is in the fact that the casino is getting a bigger slice of your wins than just the occasional 12. However, buying the numbers five, nine, four and 10 for the amounts indicated and placing the six and eight at $60 will give you a good game and a high rating.

The Captain: "These new buy bets are the optimum buys of those numbers. The house has the least possible edge on them when you're place betting However, if you decide to increase your bets on the four and 10 to $59 for a two dollar tax, the house is beginning to get back what you had previously stripped away - its big edge. I don't recommend escalating these bets unless you're in the midst of a torrid roll and you don't mind giving over a little more of your win to the casino. For comping purposes, bets of $38, $39, and $60 are more than enough to put you in the high roller category for most casinos. The total combined bet is $137 if you have the four, five and six. Usually the casinos like to see approximately $150 of action per bet, which you will surpass every time two of your numbers are the six and eight. So if you want to be a high roller but still attempt to cut the house edge and win, then play one of the two methods above. But remember to call your bets off if they aren't hitting. In the casino ratings game, you are not going to be deprived of your comps when you occasionally call off your bets. Remember that your body is still at the table earning time!"

There is one other buy bet that should be mentioned in this chapter. It is rarely found, and currently Binions Horseshoe is the only casino I've played in recently that offers it. In this buy, you pay the tax *after* and *only* on a *win!* And at Binions, you can buy the four or 10 for as little as five dollars. When you win on such a bet, you will receive your $10 win minus the five percent tax on the initial bet. If you are a place/buy bettor, this is a wonderful game.

Strongest minds
Are often those of whom the noisy world
Hears least.

...Wordsworth

Chapter Seven

The Oddsmen (and Women) of Craps

Casinos are in business to make money and anything even remotely resembling a fair shake for the player is simply there as a lure to get you to play and, hopefully, lose. That's a given. Of course, there are smarter and dumber players. The smart players play low house percentage bets, hoping that in the short-term fluctuations of chance, these low percentages can be overcome and small wins accumulated. The dumb players play on a whim, a wish, and a hope.

Critics of casino gambling would never distinguish smart from dumb players. To them, anyone who bets on a negative expectation, however slight, is dumb. What they would say is that the hierarchy of gambling intelligence goes from somewhat dumb all the way down to extremely dumb. In their estimation, and mythology, everyone who gambles must lose in the long run. It's an article of faith that a man such as the Captain, who beats a negative expectation game, can't really exist. The "purist," be he a rigid mathematician or a rigid rector, would look at the casino's one in 36 edge on the 12 and not consider it the price of admission for an other -

wise fair game, as does the Captain, but rather as an anchor, heavy enough to ultimately sink the Captain's ship.

Indeed, it is uncommon for a player to turn the tables on the casinos. We shouldn't resent the casinos for turning a profit on the desire of the common man or woman to waltz with Dame Fortune or lambada with Lady Luck. After all, if everyone were like the Captain and the casinos lost money, they wouldn't be there and then who would you dance with? The common man thinks: "Who knows? Tonight Dame Fortune may become my love slave and I'll take home oodles and oodles of cash!"

Casinos are fun places, first and foremost, and for the overwhelming majority of people, gambling is a harmless but thrilling form of entertainment. And there is no more thrilling game than craps. Just listen to the roars and moans coming from the craps tables on your next visit to a casino. Just feel your heart race as you place those bets at risk and the shooter is fixing the dice in preparation for his roll.

However, there is a method of play that even the purist priests of probability can't condemn; a form of play that actually wipes out the entire *mathematical* edge of the casino.

The Captain: "I have my tongue firmly planted in my cheek when I call this form of betting the *oddsman* betting system, because you have to be a little odd, in a nice way mind you, to play this way.

"I say you have to be odd because unlike the usual craps bet where you put your money at risk and then hope and holler, the oddsman bet requires a personality to pull off. If you wish to become an oddsman or woman you must be possessed of grace, charm, intuition and good timing. These qualities are not found in everyone."

The Captain occasionally plays the oddsman's game. The people who play this way are an interesting lot. Unlike your typical craps player who plants himself in a given spot at a given table, the oddsmen and women roam the tables looking for that perfect bet. If they don't find it at one place, they'll go to another casino. These folks are serious craps players and refuse to let the casino have even a tiny edge on the them.

Here's the bet.

Look for a person with a Pass Line bet up without the odds behind it. Then simply ask him or her if you "could place some odds behind the line."

That's correct. Many players, for whatever their personal reasons, don't take the odds on many of their Pass Line bets. The oddsman figures: "Why let a perfect betting opportunity go to waste?" So he takes the odds.

The Captain: "Once an oddsman's bet is on the table, he has the best betting situation possible for a craps player. First, he gets the true odds on his bet without giving the casino even a tiny nibble at his bankroll. More importantly, he has discretionary removal of the bet. The reason place bettors pay a heavy tax on their bets is for just such discretionary removal. The Pass Line and Come bets cannot be removed once they're on a number because the casino has a big edge on those bets once they're up. This makes up for the fact that when you first put a Pass Line or Come bet up you have eight ways of winning and just four ways of losing out of 36 possible results. Once the Pass Line and Come bets go on a number, the odds swing wildly in the casino's favor because they only pay off at even money.

"By betting the oddsman way, you aren't stuck with a particular number either. If the Pass Line number is six or eight, you may decide to go up on it. But perhaps you don't want to risk it if it's a four or 10. You have choices and an even game.

"If you do not have the patience to play the Supersystem because it means staying in one place too long and if you like to roam, this could be the method for you. You can get into the action but you can get into at any betting level you choose. Remember, even if the person has, say, a $100 bet on the Pass Line in a double odds game, you don't have to put $200 behind it. You could put $10 behind.

"This approach to craps allows you a flexibility that the casinos don't offer. You can set your minimum bets, get a fair game, and discretionary removal. If your personality is suited to this, it is a wonderful way to approach the game of craps. Combined with the *5-Count,* it can give the player an advantage hitherto unheard of in this mathematically challenging game."

Although it's a great way to bet, it is not the easiest bet to place. Many craps players are a cantankerous lot and will look upon someone wanting to place odds behind their Pass Line bet with suspicion.

The Captain: "It's an art to be able to ask total strangers if you can take advantage of a situation that they themselves are not taking advantage of. You have to gracious and non-threatening. But you also have to act as if this is an established way of playing, like placing a bet on someone else's betting circle in blackjack as is common in Asia. Don't act as if this is an unusual request.

"From my experience, women have an easier time of getting this bet down than men. A female member of my Crew has about a 75 percent success rate in getting this bet down. I have about a 50 percent success rate.

"Being an oddsman requires the ability of reading the people who are playing. You have to know which people to approach. As a general rule women are more open to the bet than men, younger women are more open than older women who tend to get more flustered when approached; novices to craps are more open than veterans. Next, younger men are more open than older men, and sober men are more open, and a hell of a lot nicer, than drinkers."

Now, if you wanted to take advantage of this bet what would you do?

The Captain: "Never go to a table that's packed, because you'll irritate the players when you push your way in. Look for a table that has action but has some room. Make sure you have your chips in hand as you approach the table. If you see someone with a Pass Line bet and no odds quickly scan the table to see if there are some Come bets on the numbers. This will indicate if the shooter has made some rolls before your arrival. If there are two Come bets showing, then wait one roll before politely asking the person if you can place the odds behind his Pass Line. Sometimes I explain that I'm not going to be playing long and I just want to get in on the action. You'd be surprised how often this works."

Where are the best places to look for this betting opportunity?

The Captain: "In Las Vegas, for some reason, there are a substantial number of craps players who don't like to take the odds, especially behind the four or 10. Also, in Vegas, there are a number of casinos that offer 10 times odds. Here, because of limited bankrolls, players will not place the full odds behind the Pass Line. It is not unusual to see someone with a five dollar Pass Line bet and no odds at a 10 times odds table! That's a potential $50 you can place as a bet with the house having no edge on you whatsoever.

"Naturally, you do have to be careful who you ask. I once asked this grizzled, old desert type at Binions in downtown Las Vegas and he said yes. I should have known better by his beer breath. So when I won the bet, he scooped up the chips. I couldn't convince him that those were my chips behind his bet, not his! I've learned from experience the look of someone who will not only say yes but remember it afterwards.

"Some casinos are better than others for locating good oddsman bets. Casinos offering three, four, five or 10 times odds will have more betting opportunities than casinos offering double odds. That's because some people just don't want to part with the extra cash necessary for placing the odds behind their bets."

So the next time you're wandering around the craps tables, give a look and see if everyone is taking full advantage of the odds. If not, consider becoming an oddsman or woman. It's a perfectly rational way to approach the game of craps. I mean, what's so odd about a person wanting to get an even game?

Nothing great was ever achieved without enthusiasm.

...Ralph Waldo Emerson

Chapter Eight

Fixing the Dice and Shooter Comportment

An area of constant controversy in gambling circles concerns the purported ability of some people to control the outcome of a dice roll. Some pundits say this ability is impossible to have; others are firm believers in the ability of certain players to control the dice.

Win Magazine, a national gaming publication, in its mid-summer 1992 issue, published the following response of a casino manager to the question of whether or not the fixing or setting of the dice can help some players control the outcome of their rolls. Responding to a complaint by a reader who had not been allowed to fix the dice before his roll when he played at the Pioneer Club in downtown Vegas, *Win Magazine's* editors contacted the casino manager, Bob Diullo, who stated: "'We know there are certain players who can set the dice, hook 'em in the corner and hit numbers, so we don't allow them to set the dice at any time.'"

You will not find this attitude at every casino. Most casinos will allow you to fix the dice as long as you can do it relatively quickly. The casino just doesn't want the game slowed down - unless *they* are doing the slowing, which as you know, will occur when someone is having a blisteringly hot roll.

I've experienced both ends of the casino "fixing" and "slowing" comportment issue. When I first started fixing my dice in the three-three "V" shape, I was a little slow. I had to look for the threes to find them. Now, I don't. Whatever side of the dice I see, I know immediately where the threes are. But in my novice days, it took a little time. Unfortunately, I went to Binions in downtown Vegas in the summer of 1990 to practice my "fixation." Well, if it wasn't the dealer, it was the floorman; if it wasn't the floorman, it was the pit boss, constantly getting on me to "stop fixin' the dice and throw!" They even threatened to take the dice away from me. I thought *they thought* that I could control the dice. No such thing. I was slowing down the game! And I never even had a decent roll. I was just taking an indecently long time by their standards to "throw the damned dice!"

Yet, in the summer of 1992, having become a lightning fixer, I was having a hot roll and, as the Captain relates in Chapter Two, the casino started to get a little concerned. After each roll, the boxman examined the dice; then they brought out the chip racks and plunked them in the middle of the table so I had to roll around them when they finally decided to let me continue my roll. The table hadn't lost enough money to warrant a new supply of five and 25 dollar chips. The majority of the players were playing dollars! But this slowed down the game. Then a dealer started to question me on every bet. "Is that your Do and Don't? How about that one?" Luckily, the even-tempered A.P. turned to the dealer and said: "Don't worry, I'm watching his bets."

There should, of course, be a general comportment agreement based upon an unwritten code, much like the social contract, that a shooter can fix the dice anyway he chooses if he can do it in a reasonable time - say, six seconds, one for each side of a die - and that the casinos will instruct their dealers and floormen and pit bosses not to harass a shooter about hitting the back wall if he only misses it *once in a row* on rare occasions, nor interrupt his roll to ask him questions ("So, sir, will the United States go the way of ancient Rome as Professor Kennedy asserts?"), or bring out chip racks in the midst of a roll, but rather wait until a roll has ended to take care of business. Also, pit crews should not be allowed to glare at civilized but hot-rolling players, and, please fellas, no more voodoo dolls! However, if a person can control the dice...well, let's hope the pits don't notice it, and players should never tell.

Does the Captain believe that certain people can control the dice?

The Captain: "Absolutely. Even if I didn't know it for a fact, I'd be very skeptical of anyone rejecting out of hand the possibility of someone not being able to do it. That would be like rejecting out of hand the possibility that someone can walk a tightrope, do card tricks, be a sharp shooter, sleep on a bed of nails, walk on red-hot coals, and a host of other abilities people develop that the average person cannot do and therefore thinks impossible. So if it's a physical talent, a combination of skill and practice, then without even researching it, I'd say yes, some people probably can do it.

"Luckily, I don't need to guess. I know that some people have trained themselves either privately or at the tables to control the fall of the dice. 'The Arm,' [see: *Beat the Craps Out of the Casinos: How to Play Craps and Win!*] has had remarkable success fixing and controlling the dice. 'The Arm' consistently has major rolls. Recently at the Sands in Atlantic City, during a Sinatra weekend, with the place packed with free-wheeling high rollers, and then several days later at the Claridge right across the street, 'The Arm' had monster rolls of positively legendary proportions. This isn't coincidence or merely fluctuations in randomness. 'The Arm' controls the dice.

"Does it mean that every time 'The Arm' picks up those cubes, a big one is coming? Of course not. There are times when she isn't at the right 'spot' on the table, or the throw is a little off. Having played with 'The Arm' for years, I can recognize the signs of an off night. So can she. But if the groove isn't there, just like a pitcher, 'The Arm' leaves the game and does not roll.

"When we talk about fixing and controlling the dice, we aren't looking for perfection. Pitchers don't pitch perfect games every time out. In fact, each separate roll of the dice to a player who can control them is like a pitch in a game. The good pitchers will consistently throw strikes and have good games, not every time out, but enough that you can say this isn't just randomness or luck. Also, you have to define what you mean by a good roll. My definition is simple: a good roll is one where the seven doesn't show long enough to make me money or one where I can make a good profit because there's a rapid succession of repeating numbers. Fixing and controlling the dice has more to do with certain numbers being repeated than it does with monster rolls. You don't have to have monster rolls to win. I've seen rolls by 'The Arm' where the four will come up four or five times in a row, followed by some other numbers, then another string of fours before a sevening out. It's a wonderful feeling to be up on only one number after the *5-Count* and have that number hit repeatedly in rapid succession. People who can control the dice will tend to have certain faces of the dice appear more often than these faces would otherwise by chance."

By now everyone who reads gambling books has probably run across some version of the story about the eccentric college professor who practiced his dice throw in his basement for 10 years until he could, with a dazzling degree of regularity, get one of the dice to come up with the one-face showing. The second die did whatever it did and each face came up however often it came up. What this meant was that the two (1:1) had as much chance of showing as did a seven (6:1). Even if he could only get the die to appear on the one a third of the time, he would be paid 30 to one by betting "snake eyes." Needless to say, when this man descended on Las Vegas, the casinos didn't know what hit them. But, as they always do when someone seems to know how to win, the casinos took immediate action; the professor was quickly banned from playing craps and he has since vanished into gambling folklore.

Now, his case is rare because of two things: the incredible degree of consistency in his rolls and the fact that the regulation craps tables in those days used to have *flat* back walls, which made it easier to control the rebound. Since then, the casinos have taken counter measures and made the back walls with foam rubber pyramids protruding from them. These pyramids are there to randomize the rolls. When the dice hit today's back walls, the rebound is supposedly impossible to predict. That's why the pit crews are almost paranoid when you fail to hit the back wall because they think you are derandomizing the game. Despite these precautions, some people can still control the dice well enough to get a slight edge over the casino. That's all you need.

The Captain: "I fix the dice but I don't really have control over them. Sometimes I have good rolls, sometimes I don't. I fix the dice because I enjoy it and I like the feeling that I might be able to influence the roll somewhat by my fixing of them. But I don't pretend to have control of the outcome.

"I know what is necessary, however, in order to at least have a shot at controlling them. You have to put in the time, probably hundreds, if not thousands of hours, developing your physical mechanics. You'll have to work on the initial fixing of the dice by analyzing thousands of rolls when you fix the dice this way or that way. Then you'll have to develop your throw: fast, slow. Will the dice spin or tumble? The popular wisdom is that one of the dice must spin, not tumble, for a given face to come up more frequently than it should.

"When you practice, you have to analyze each die. Use two different colors and always position the colors the same way. If you are positioning the dice one on top of the other, then the same color must always be on the bottom. You must keep a record of your results for each die, not in terms of the combined number that is thrown, but in terms of the faces that appear.

"Personally, I don't have the time or the patience to do such an exercise, especially since there is no guarantee that I'll succeed. How many people want to be great major league pitchers? But how many people actually do it, even after years of practice? Not many. There will be individuals who have the talent to control the dice and with practice and desire they can develop that talent. I'm not one of them. But you might be.

"The other impediment for most people flirting with this endeavor is the fact that you must practice on a regulation table. Now, that's an expense. Also, there are several table sizes that are considered regulation. You'll probably have to decide, based on some research, which table most frequently appears in casinos and buy that one. To a determined person none of these problems will present an obstacle. So go out, get that regulation table, develop your mechanics until you've hit upon the method that works for you, and then take millions from the casinos. But before you do, write to the publisher of this book and let us all know where you'll be playing. We'll even put up some bets for the shooter!"

In addition to a regulation table and regulation dice, you have to have some formula by which to judge your results. Obviously, you're going to have to experiment with various "fixes" and "throws." Thus, for each "fix and throw," an initial trial of 6,000 rolls would be sufficient to *suggest* further practice with this method. What results are you looking for?

Probability theory predicts that for every throw of a single die each face has a one in six chance of appearing. Thus, in 6,000 throws each face should *theoretically* appear

1,000 times. I say theoretically because there isn't a chance in a million that in 6,000 throws each and every face will appear exactly 1,000 times. There will be variations. Some faces will appear more than others. This could simply be the result of random fluctuations.

You have to develop a confidence rating for your rolls. A strong confidence rating means that your rolling technique has *caused* certain faces to appear more often. A weak confidence rating means it's unclear whether certain faces have appeared more often due to chance or due to technique. This is for a single die. Here is a guideline for developing a confidence rating. For 6,000 rolls of the dice, a face appearing 1,400 to 1,800 times would indicate that you are controlling the dice. Less than 1,150 could merely be due to randomness. I would do several 6,000 run trials after a positive confidence rating appeared because you want to be sure of your ability when you enter the casino and put your money at risk.

Once you have your confidence rating, decide how to bet it. If the one-face is showing more often on one die than any other face, is it worth your while to bet that the two will appear more than its probable once in 36 times? The casino has a heavy edge on this bet. Is your roll enough to overcome the edge? It certainly is if the one-face is showing up a third of the time. That's the equivalent of having one die with two one-faces. That means that the two will come up twice every 36 rolls, or once every 18 rolls. That's 17 to one. The payoff is 30 to one. Great bet! A 30 to one payoff on an 17 to one shot. You'll have to work on this mathematical aspect of your game should you develop a high confidence rating in a given face. What would you do if the three-face is consistently showing half of the time? Would a hard six be a good bet? How about any combination of numbers with a three - on the hop!? (A "hop" bet is a one roll bet where you call what number or combination you're betting on. There is no indication of this bet on the layout.) So you'd call out: "Three/one on the hop! Three/two on the hop! Three/three on the hop! Three/four on the hop! Three/five on the hop! And three/six on the hop! And make it quick!" as you drop a pile of chips on the table. You can always dream. But, like the Captain, I believe that controlling the dice is an achievable dream for a select, and driven, few. The rest of us will have to be content to occasionally get into a rhythmic roll and go with the flow.

If you pick up a starving dog and make him prosperous, he will not bite you. This is the principal difference between a dog and a man.

...Mark Twain

## Chapter Nine

The Captain On:
Table Selection,
Don't Betting,
Tipping,
The "Negatives" of
Supersystem Play
and
Gambling in General

Since the publication of *Beat the Craps Out of the Casinos: How to Play Craps and Win!*, I have received many letters of reaction and commentary from craps players, requests to meet the Captain, and questions directed towards the Captain.

One highly unflattering letter was from a dealer friend of mine in Las Vegas who had given the book to some casino bosses and they *hated* it! I mean, they *really hated* it. Good. Although it might hurt sales of my books because casinos won't put them in their gift shops, I'm flattered that the reactions were so strong. (Did you ever wonder how good the gambling books in casinos' gift shops are if the casinos allow them to be sold? Or how good the advice is of a "gambling authority" if the casinos hire him to hold seminars and workshops for their players in their meeting rooms? If the "gambling authority" could help the players win, would the very same casinos *that ban card counters* allow him to run seminars and workshops?)

Many of the questions writers asked me have been answered within the context of this book already. The three areas that came up most frequently in the letters written to me concerned table selection, Don't betting, and tipping. Some readers also wanted a fuller explanation of what could go wrong with the Supersystem, so they could be more prepared for a losing session. I have taken the gist of these various letters and boiled them down into a question in each category for the Captain to answer. Lastly, the Captain will have some thoughts on gambling in general.

Table Selection

Is it true that some tables are better for playing than others? If so, how do you decide what's a good table and what's a bad table? I read another craps author who says he spends a good couple of hours tracking tables. Is this a good idea?

The Captain: "I don't think it's necessary to spend hours watching tables in order to select one to play at. If you have a lot of time to kill and you enjoy watching games, then go ahead and do it. Most people who go to Atlantic City are lucky to find a spot at any table, particularly on the crowded weekends. The common wisdom is that technically any table is as good as any other table since craps is a random game of independent trials. The dice have no memory so how can a table be 'hot' or 'cold?' Intellectually, this idea is true. However, human beings are intuitive as well as rational creatures. So I say this: if it really doesn't matter what table you play at then *why not* go with your intuitive feelings? It can't hurt and it might help.

"So here's what to look for to pick a table. You won't have to spend hours hunting either. I look for a table where people are either happy or, at least, not cursing and moaning. If the people are happy it's a good bet they are winning or, at least, not losing. To me this means that shooters are sevening out long after the *5-Count* and I'll be able to get in on the action. If the people are not cursing and moaning and groaning, it probably means that the table is a little choppy but no one is getting hurt too badly. These two tables I would play at. Given a choice, I'd obviously pick a happy table. There's another reason for this. You might have a rhythmic roller or several of them at one table. If you should overhear comments like: 'Boy, that lady has had three good rolls already!' this table might be really worth a look.

"I would also look to see if there are any Don't bettors at a table. If there are two or three Don't bettors and their chip racks seem full and they seem happy, I'd pass the table on by. You might have a shooter or several shooters who are rhythmic seven rollers.

"If you are a Don't bettor, the reverse would be true. Look for a table of Don't bettors who are happy. Keep your ears open for comments like: 'This table is ice cold!' 'We gotta get a shooter!' and 'I'm getting killed!' would indicate that this table has been a Don't player's delight.

"Once you pick a table, as a Supersystem player you would stay with it as long as players are sevening out within the *5-Count.* If the table should change and you suddenly find yourself losing within a roll or two of putting your money at risk, then go to another table. At risk means your odds are on. Once you've lost a third of your session stake, go to another table.

"If you are winning, stay until you lose on a shooter or two before calling it a session. After a big roll, too many craps players hang around and lose what they've won. Get out as soon as you lose a couple of times.

"Never lose an entire session stake at one table. That's a law. Don't allow yourself to get clobbered at one table. Move. If you're lucky you'll go to the next table and start to win. Sometimes you won't find another table. So quit for an hour and go for a walk. Or place a couple of oddsman bets and see what happens.

"When you approach a table and see that there are several Come bets with odds on them, start the placing Come and Don't Come as if it were the 3-Count. Once you have two numbers working, take the odds.

"Again, intellectually table selection is of no use because craps is supposed to be a random game. But what if it isn't? What if the table you're approaching has a shooter who can control the dice? See all those happy faces? My intuition tells me I'd rather play there than at that other table where they're cursing and moaning."

Don't Betting

You're a right bettor and almost all your systems and advice are based on betting right. How about wrong bettors? Can the Supersystem be employed for wrong betting purposes? Or is there a better way? Right now I place a Don't Pass bet and lay full odds. Should I place a Pass Line and a Don't Pass instead and then take the full odds?

The Captain: "You're right, as a general rule, I'm not a wrong bettor. I prefer to bet with the shooter. I play craps to make money, but I also play for the almost primitive tribal feelings that can develop as everyone roots for everyone else. I am from the old school emotionally, I must admit. Although I try not to, I find that when I'm rolling if someone bets against me I get irritated and I take pleasure in making my point and seeing him lose. That is of course totally at odds with logic but that's the way I feel.

"However, there are times when I bet wrong. In games with single odds or on some cruise ships, or when a table is ice, ice cold and almost everyone is betting wrong, I will, too.

"As I see it, there are seven ways to approach wrong betting.

"1.) Place a Don't Pass bet against the shooter and, when you're up, place full odds against the point.

"2.) Place a Don't Pass and when you're up *don't* lay any odds against the point.

"3.) Place a Pass Line and a Don't Pass bet, which will protect you against the seven and eleven on the come out, and then lay the odds against the point.

"4.) Place a Don't Come or several Don't Come bets and when you're up on the numbers lay the odds against them.

"5.) Place a Don't Come or several Don't Come bets and *don't* lay odds against the numbers.

"6.) Place a Come and Don't Come bet or several Come and Don't Come bets and lay against the numbers when you're up on them.

"7.) Do a straight lay bet against one or more numbers.

"It's appropriate that there are seven ways to view Don't betting because the seven is a boon and a bust for the Don't bettor. If you place a Don't Pass bet and the shooter rolls a series of sevens and elevens, you can find yourself in a hole quickly. How often have you seen a shooter come out with sevens and elevens blazing? It happens quite often, believe me.

"Now, let's say that you get past the come out without getting hurt. If you don't lay odds against the number, you are in the driver's seat because you're getting an even money payoff on a bet where you have either a six to five, three to two, or two to one advantage. Once you're up on the number, by laying odds against the number, you're laying out more money but you aren't increasing your advantage. The odds game is merely an even game. Why go to an even game when you have a big advantage? It doesn't make sense. It makes does make sense on the Do side, it doesn't make sense on the Don't side. So why bother putting up more money? Do on the Do and don't on the Don't is a simple formula for odds betting.

"I do believe come out rolls can be devastating to a Don't Pass bettor. So one way to attempt to protect yourself is to play both sides on the come out and then lay the odds. This is a form of the Supersystem *if* and *only if* you adhere to the *5-Count* by taking down your odds bet or reversing it should the shooter achieve the *5-Count*. Personally, I don't like this because you are placing too much money at risk too quickly. A cold shooter is still cold even if he makes a point and then sevens out. But you've lost in the interim.

"Forget about simply laying or place betting against the numbers because the house takes a healthy bite out of your wins just as it does on the right side of place betting.

"To me, the best way to play wrong is on the Don't Come. A shooter can't hurt you with a string of sevens because the very first seven is the end of his roll. Then a new shooter has to come out. So one shooter can only hurt you a little. He can nail you with the seven when you place your initial Don't Come bet. Then he's done for on the seven because he's done for on his roll. He can nail you with a one in 18 chance of the 11 on the initial Don't Come also. But you can win on the two and three, which combined are a one in 12 chance. So a rhythmic seven-shooter only gets one shot at you. As soon as you're up on the number, the advantage shifts dramatically to you, just as it does on the Don't Pass. And, again, I would not lay the odds. Nor would I play the Doey-Don't and lay the odds, unless I was willing to switch to the Do side on the *5-Count*.

"I would just play one, two, or three Don't Come numbers and let it go at that. And if a shooter started to make numbers, I would not keep putting up Don't Come bets. I'd either revert to the Supersystem or wait out the shooter if I were an inveterate Don't type. It's hard to make dramatic comebacks on the Don't side of betting because the best payoffs are simply even money. You have to win a lot of bets on the Don't side, if you've gotten yourself in a hole, to get even. So don't let a single shooter ever put you in a hole. Only place a couple of Don't Come bets and if one shooter hits those numbers again, take your small loss and wait for another shooter. If several shooters have hurt you, go to another table where people are complaining about how bad things are.

"As you can see my Don't betting thoughts are colored by my belief that a come-out shooter is the most dangerous shooter in the long run for a Don't bettor. So avoid this shooter. You really can't be clobbered on the Don't Come unless a shooter rolls several elevens in a row, an unlikely event. You can only lose once on the seven or once if he hits that number again. You can't be clobbered by one shooter shooting a sequence of sevens as you can on the Don't Pass bet. If a shooter looks as if he's getting hot, don't bet against him. Either wait him out or go with the Supersystem.

"I would also recommend that you not play a Martingale on the Don't Come if you should lose a bet. A Martingale is a double-your-bet-after-a-loss system. Take your losses in small doses on the Don't Come side of the table. If you're winning, then increase your bets gradually. Personally, I would never lay odds against the number on my Don't Come bets.

"Mathematically, there is no difference between a Don't Pass and a Don't Come. However, mathematics can't take into consideration a seven-shooter on the come out. My *eyes* can take them into consideration because my eyes have *seen* them often enough to convince my intuition that a Don't bettor's best bet is on the Don't Come without laying odds."

Tipping

How much and how often should you tip craps dealers? How should you tip them? Having played the Supersystem for almost a year now, I can tell that not many dealers like the amount of work they have to do. Will a tip help?

The Captain: "I've done something of an about-face concerning tipping and I owe it all to a member of my Crew. She makes a simple but powerful case for tipping dealers and tipping them relatively early when you're playing. Her reasoning goes like this: the dealers are minimum wage workers for the most part, like waiters, waitresses, valet parkers, and so forth, and they perform a service just as those other workers do. For that service, they should be tipped since tipping is their main income. For players playing the Supersystem, you are asking the dealers to do an unaccustomed amount of work, so an early tip, perhaps as you're shooting, will go a long way towards making them pleasant and helpful.

"Now, I used to tip at the end of a session if the dealers were friendly. I found that often enough they were surly. However, I have started tipping relatively early in my play and I have found the dealers to be much more pleasant and helpful. If mistakes *happen* to be made at my table, they tend to favor me. (A rule of thumb at a craps game is to never tell a dealer he's made a mistake that *favors* you, by the way, because that would embarrass him and he might not make that mistake for you again.) Also, the dealers will keep track of your bets for you and remind you to take odds if you've forgotten. In addition, when you call off your bets on occasion, they'll hear you readily.

"So I've begun to place a hardways bet for them. Another Supersystem playing Crew member places a two-way hard eight, figuring if it hits he'll be in on it too. He does this only when he's shooting because he says that he tends to roll the four on his left die more than usual. He hasn't done a confidence study of it yet (his craps table is on order) but he says he seems to hit the hard eight early in his rolls. He too has seen a dramatic change in the attitudes of most dealers after he gets that initial tip out.

"You can decide how you want to tip. The hardways aren't good bets but if they hit for the dealers, they get a good payoff. You also don't have to put up very much, even a dollar will do. The dealers will appreciate it and I think you'll see better treatment of you and your bets."

The "Negatives" of Supersystem Play

Most books and systems sellers spend so much time explaining the good points of their systems that they forget to remind readers that it is still possible to lose. Is the Supersystem flawless? What can go wrong with it? What do you do when things aren't going right?

The Captain: "You're right about most books and systems sellers lingering on the positive aspects of their methods and relegating the negative statements to single sentences designed to cover them should their readers or buyers lose. There's a different reason why I personally tend not to linger on the negative. I assume most intelligent craps players know exactly how to lose. After all, they've experienced enough losses to know about them.

"But it is good to know what can go wrong with the Supersystem, so that when it happens, and it will happen, you won't panic. Remember, the Supersystem is a *cut* and *position* way to play. You want to *cut* your losses due to horrendous rolls and you want to *position* yourself to take advantage of good rolls by keeping your losses low enough to make a profit when the good rolls do come along. It is a grinding method of play and quite often you will be spending quite a bit of time at tables without risking any money. That's good because if your money is not at risk for any extended period of time, it means the table is cold and people are losing. The Doey-Don't method of betting gives you an almost even game so that the casino can't get you into a huge hole just based on the mathematics.

"But you can lose at certain types of tables. These are the Supersystem nightmare scenarios.

"You get up on three or four numbers, the *5-Count* is completed, and now you tell the dealer as you lay a mound of chips on the table: 'I'm taking maximum odds on all my Come bets!' The next roll and you hear the dealer shout: 'Seven! Seven out!' You've just been blown away. You've lost three or four bets on a single roll.

"If this happens twice in rapid succession, go to another table and take your time about it. Clear your head and control your anxieties before entering the fray again. If you lose six to eight craps bets on just two rolls, you need six to eight rolls of *just your numbers hitting* to get back up to even or just a little bit ahead. The worst thing to do in a situation like this is press. Don't bet more. If anything bet less or take a little time off.

"Although it has happened infrequently to me, it is conceivable that you could get blown away four or five times in succession, first at one table, then at another, then another and so forth. Quit for the day. There is no guarantee that tomorrow will be any better, but my experience is that when things are going badly on a given day, they keep going badly. That's why you have to give yourself a certain set amount to lose and stick to it. Never lose more than that amount. Never.

"Most craps players have gotten themselves into such deep holes in their playing careers that they'd need a roll lasting months to just get even. Don't get into a big hole on one day. Spread out your play from day to day as well as table to table and casino to casino. In this way, it would have to be a bad streak of epic dimensions to hurt you in the long run. My experience has been that a few days might be nightmarish but by spreading out the pain from table to table, casino to casino, and ultimately day to day, keeping to my predetermined loss limits, I weather the storm and come roaring back.

"Here's the next nightmare case. You're up on three or four numbers and the shooter rolls three or four times without hitting your number. You take your bets off. Now, the shooter hits one of your numbers. It comes off. You place a Doey-Don't bet. On the second roll, the shooter makes the same number. Now, you're up on it and your bets are working. The shooter now rolls several times and once again doesn't hit your numbers. Off you go. Once again he hits the numbers when you're off them. This goes back and forth. The shooter now sevens out with you up on your three or four numbers and all of them are working. You didn't win a bet, although your numbers kept hitting while you were off them.

"This happens on occasion. It is not as frequent as being blown away on the sixth or seventh roll, but it does happen. If it happens a few times at the same table, go to another table, or play the Radical Supersystem and stay working as you chase the numbers. If this doesn't work, get out of the game, maybe even out of the casino for a while.

"I realize that this *leave the table litany* is standard advice. But it's good advice. I know there is no guarantee that a new table will be any better but you will *feel* better getting away from the source of pain. When I get hurt at a table, I'll move just so I don't have to feel the pain. Gambling is emotional. Go to a new table. You'll feel better. You'll be able to think clearly, too. How often have you experienced a lousy run, stayed, got upset, pressed your bets, got blown away, pressed some more and finally lost everything? Spread it out. Don't keep getting clobbered at the same locale. Move. At the very least, moving around will allow you a moment of reflection: 'Should I continue? Or should I take a nap? Maybe I'll take a nap.'

The next case is more subtle. You win a few and you lose a few more. Win a few, lose a few more. The table is grinding you down. You aren't being blown out, and you aren't experiencing two awful events in sequence, so you aren't fully aware that if this keeps up you are going to experience a blood bath. Always be aware of your money. After each shooter sevens out, take a count of your bankroll. If you notice that you have lost a third of your session stake, once again I say: 'Move to another table.'

"As you are losing, always try to play variations of the Supersystem. If the Radical Supersystem isn't winning, go with the Classic. If you are betting aggressively, slow down and get a little conservative. Bet less and maybe spread to more numbers. Bet more and have fewer numbers working. Maybe look for a single win on your standard bet and once that happens, go down to a smaller odds bet until it hits again. You have to react to situations analytically. Try different things. But whatever you do, don't let your emotions control your experimenting. Always make high percentage bets. Always played a controlled game.

Finally, the worst scenario is to combine all the aforementioned with a Crazy Crapper at your table who bets every stupid bet imaginable and hits them! You're playing a brilliantly controlled game, using the ultimate craps system, and this bozo is guffawing as he puts up one stupid bet after another and wins! Your bankroll is being whittled away. His is exploding. The only thing you can do is shake your head and realize that even the idiots have their moments and that bad players can have good days, too. (You can still hate the guy, however.)

Some Thoughts on Gambling

The Captain: "I have been gambling all my lifetime, be it in business ventures or games of chance and skill. In my youth, I made every mistake a gambler could make. That's how most of us learn. If a gambler doesn't learn, he destroys himself and those around him.

"I know why I gamble. I like winning money first off. But I also like the thrill. There's nothing wrong in enjoying the rush that comes with risking money - if you can afford it. I think that most people who enjoy gambling think of it as a manageable risk. They don't want to risk their actual lives, as does a mountain climber or sky diver, for the thrill, so they risk a part of their economic life on it. They can afford the loss but they bet just enough to make a loss painful and a win thrilling. It's a wonderful outlet.

"It's also a challenge. I've given up new investments in most other forms of gambling, the horses, stocks, real estate, and so forth. The biggest gamble, getting married, paid off well. I've been happily married to the same woman for 46 years. The second biggest gamble, having kids, was also a good bet. Genetics is worse than a craps game and back in all our pasts are relatives we'd rather not see coming out in our kids. So I've been most lucky in the two most important areas of life. So far as genetics, I'm still on a good roll as my four grandchildren are great thus far too. What more could a man ask for?

"Craps is a lot like life, only faster. It's a sifting down to the bare essentials: man taking risks to get what he wants. Of course, it is not an important enterprise in the grand scheme of things. It's just a game. I know that primitive man would roll dice made of bone to ask the gods' favor or opinion and read in the results a yeah or nay to his plans and aspirations. I'm somewhat superstitious as some of my intuitions and opinions will attest. But I don't think of craps or any gambling as a message from the gods. It's fun; it's a challenge; and if you can win, it's a feeling of triumph, especially if you're not *supposed* to win because the casinos have stacked the game in their favor.

"I don't think gambling is evil. I think that people who can't control their gambling impulses are the same types who take up long distance running and run so far so fast so often that they injure themselves physically and take so much time away from their loved ones they might as well be dead. The person who tends to get out of control will get out of control on something or other, even if gambling never existed.

"So as a manageable thrill, gambling is one outlet that I would recommend, if you can keep yourself controlled. It's a good test of character too. How people handle a loss is a good indication of what they're made of. Just look around a casino on your next visit and it's a study in character. You could pick the people you would want to depend on based upon their reactions at gaming table. I know I would never trust someone who was unwilling to gamble, even just a little, because non-risk takers are bores and are quite unreliable. I like the gleam in the eye of a person who is willing to take a chance, win or lose, succeed or fail. Those are my kind of people, my kind of crew, and I welcome them aboard my ship."

*There is no such thing as absolute certainty, but there is
assurance sufficient for the purposes of human life.*

...John Stuart Mill

## Chapter Ten

Some Thoughts on Randomness and Probability

I have always been interested in randomness and probability. I'm not quite sure they exist in the real world as we perceive of them or think of them in theory. For example, I have never seen any series of random events ever conform to probability theory; that's because everything is a deviation from the norm. That's an interesting way of saying that everything is not conforming to this particular principle called the norm or expectation. So what is this norm in probability theory? The norm doesn't exist concretely in the real world. It only exists in the math. Is the math reality? No. It's a mind construct or language that attempts to reflect and predict reality. It's a shadow of reality, not the full substance.

If each face of a die is theoretically supposed to appear once every six times, then the *norm* for 6,000 rolls is each face will theoretically come up 1,000 times. But, of course, each face *won't* come up 1,000 times. In fact, it's a safe bet that not a *single* face will come up exactly 1,000 times. Maybe you didn't do enough trials? So roll the dice 6,000,000 times.

Do you think any one face will come up exactly 1,000,000 times? Don't bet on it. Some "probabilists" say that as you approach "infinity" probability will definitely apply. Of course, you can never reach or even approach infinity since, as far as we know, we are in a finite universe. But why quibble?

Yet, I recognize that given two choices, one with high probability and one with low probability, I'd rather bet on the high probability event. So I would never say that betting on a two is better than betting on the seven if the payoffs were not reflective of the true odds (probability) for making that number. That's dumb. If the shadow looks like a bear, it probably is a bear. The bear of a seven will come up *in reality* a hell of a lot more than a two and you won't have to get anywhere near infinity to ascertain this truth. In a million rolls of two dice, bet on the seven to appear somewhere *in the vicinity* of six times more frequently than the two. But will it ever be exactly six times as frequent? No. Nor will the seven appear exactly as often as probability predicts. It might appear more, it might appear less, but it almost assuredly will not appear exactly as predicted. It will be in the vicinity (more or less).

The more the actual rolls, the more closely it should conform to its theoretical expectation. In terms of a percentage it will indeed be closer to its actual expectation than away from it, *but* as an *absolute* number, it will be even further away.

I'll explain this.

Take a coin toss. Theoretically, each side should come up half the time, assuming you were flipping a perfectly balanced coin that didn't mess around by landing on its side. In the first ten throws let's say the heads comes up six times and the tails comes up four times. The heads has come up 60 percent of the time, the tails 40 percent. But only two *absolute* numbers separate them. The heads has just come up two more times that's all. No big deal.

But given a million rolls, the heads might come up 500,427 times, while the tails comes up 499,573. The heads is only coming up 50.0427 percent of the time, while the tails is coming up 49.9573 percent of the time. Not much of a percentage difference. That's pretty close, yes? No! In absolute terms, the heads has come up 854 more times. That's a pretty hefty number, especially if you are betting a $1,000 a toss.

Probability theory is not accurate, it is merely strongly *indicative*. It points up a range of results, not the actual results. For a craps player playing the Supersystem, and facing a small house edge, probability theory doesn't predict the future so much as warn you of it. In a coin toss, generally the side that is winning halfway through the throws will be winning at the end of the throws. In gambling terms, that's simply the old adage of betting the trend. In craps, it's a little more complicated because there are so many different results. However, the *5-Count* helps you avoid the devastating "trend" of getting clobbered early on the countless cold rolls you'll encounter. The Doey-Don't gives you a method of betting to take advantage of repetitious rolls with the house not sharing in the profits when your numbers hit. The casino does take its nip out of your Come or Pass bet when the 12 appears and *theoretically* in the long run, this should make you lose. But theory and the real dust and smoke world of the casinos, with players handling the dice, fixing the dice, controlling the dice are two different things. If you encounter enough rhythmic rollers and dice controllers in your play, then who has the edge in such a close contest?

I remember one time the Captain and I were strolling through the huge Tropworld Casino. We had just finished a rather successful session and we were going to enjoy our wins. As we passed a table, the Captain paused to watch. There were only three people at the table: an older couple at one end and a neatly dressed man at the other end. The woman was shooting. She sevened out. The neatly dressed man now had the dice. He rolled a point number and then sevened out at the 3-Count.

Still the Captain remained and watched. So did I. I had no idea, and I didn't ask him immediately, why he was bothering to watch an almost empty table when we already had finished playing for the night and had our wins in our pockets. I just watched and tried to figure out what he was looking for.

The man opposite the neatly dressed man rolled. He hit a seven on the come out, made a number, rolled several numbers and sevened out at the *5-Count*. The woman sevened out on the second roll. The Captain stayed. The neatly dressed man went to roll again. He sevened out on the third roll!

It went around again. The couple did not on their respective rolls get past the *5-Count*. Suddenly, the Captain took out his chips and went to the table. I did likewise. Why? I have no idea. When I play with the Captain I just do as he does. The neatly dressed man had the dice. Both the Captain and I waited for the *5-Count*. This time the neatly dressed man sevened out two rolls after the *5-Count* and we both lost three bets! At this point the couple left to look for greener pastures. The Captain and I stayed.

The Captain passed up the dice. I rolled. I got past the *5-Count* and repeated a couple of numbers, then I sevened out. It was the neatly dressed man's turn again.

He rolled for a half hour!

The Captain and I both got in on the roll after the *5-Count* and won a considerable amount.

When the neatly dressed man's roll was over, the table was only half full. Neither the Captain, the neatly dressed man, nor myself had made any fuss or noise during this exquisite roll. The Captain didn't want to disrupt the guy's rhythm by cheering, nor did he want people buying in and taking up valuable "rhythmic rolling time." This I knew.

The neatly dressed man took his chips and headed for the cage. The Captain and I followed. The Captain congratulated the man on his roll and the man smiled and said: "I thought it would never come!"

When we were alone I asked the Captain why he had watched the table and then gotten into the game?

"Instinct and *logic*," he said, emphasizing *logic*.

I asked him to explain. He did.

"I've seen that man around here and in other casinos before. He's always cool. I just happened to recognize him. I had no idea how he played or anything. So I just stopped to watch. Then I noticed certain things that I thought were interesting."

"What?" I said. I hadn't noticed anything except that the table had been cold.

"When he bet on the other shooters, he was putting $10 on the Pass Line and placing only double odds. But when he was rolling he was placing $25 on the Pass Line and taking maximum odds of three, four and five times! This was due to two things: either he just likes to bet on himself as some people do...or, this is a guy who tends to have good rolls and he knows it and he bets it up when it's his turn. So I watched his face. He wasn't too troubled when he sevened out. He just looked a little puzzled. But he was very precise in his throw and in his setting of the dice. He even took a couple of mimed practice throws before the dealer handed him the dice. So I figured if this particular shooter gets past the *5-Count*, we might have a chance. I was taking a chance that this man, who my instincts told me was obviously is not poor and not a gambling addict, knows something about himself. He knows he's a good shooter, however he does it, or knows it. So I took a gamble. If he was just an average Joe, so what? The percentages of the game don't get any worse. But if I was right, and this man is a good shooter, then if he got past the *5-Count,* I was willing to go with him." The Captain laughed: "So we lucked out!"

But it wasn't lucking out. The Captain didn't just bet with the shooter because of a *feeling*. His intuition was based on a set of cues that he assessed *might mean* the game at this particular moment was not exactly random. He played his Supersystem, waiting to see if the shooter could get past the *5-Count*. He didn't just throw bets down because of his intuition. But his intuition and *logic* told him he had a decent shot.

I've seen him do this on a number of occasions. Indeed, he has done this since the opening of Atlantic City's Resorts Casino.

The Captain's approach to craps is based on what he facetiously calls "positioning probability" and sometimes "sequential probability." These two concepts don't exist outside the Captain's humor, but to me they do mean something. If you can be in a position to take advantage of a few non-random, somewhat controlled events, and the casino doesn't have much of an edge on you going into these events, then you are in a position to win! You just have to know how to play and what to look for to *position* yourself for a winning *sequence*. The Supersystem does this for you. You certainly cannot win a fortune. But if you can win a little, a little, a little, while not losing much, after awhile you conceivably will have won a lot - certainly a lot more than you would have won had you wandered to the table like a happy idiot and bet it up.

The player also has one huge advantage over the casino. We can quit anytime we want. We don't have to bet. But the casino does. The casino must play every roll, every shooter, even he ones who are turning the percentages upside down.

We can pick our dance with Lady Luck. So given this reality, I choose to do the *5-Count* and dance to the tunes of the *Doey-Don't*. In the *real* world, the Supersystem has made the Captain a rarity, a man who makes his living dancing with Dame Fortune!

Human history becomes more and more a race between education and catastrophe.

...H.G. Wells

Appendix

In this appendix there will be some new approaches to the statistics of craps. In the section covering types of play and casino taxes, you will note that each category is based on six assumptions.

1. There are 36 perfect rolls of the dice, where every number comes up exactly as expected based on probability theory. In the real world this would never happen.

2. The seven is never used in a negative way.

3. The seven is counted in a positive way on the come out roll for Pass Line bettors.

4. For Doey-Don't bets, the initial losing 12 is counted.

5. The casino tax is the amount of money the casino takes from a win.

6. In the equalization tables all expected wins have been rounded down or up to $100 and factored accordingly. In this way, we can deal with money instead of percentages. This will give an accurate and comprehensible look at the traditionally preferred betting systems, Pass Line, Come and Place Betting as they relate to the Captain's Oddsman, Doey-Don't, and Best Buys.

(* All the following charts are based on five dollar minimum bets and the taking of full odds where appropriate.)

Oddsman Betting Method
(Any number of odds)

#	Ways to make	Money at risk	True odds	Expected win	Actual win	Casino tax
4	three	$15	2 to 1	$30	$30	0
5	four	$20	3 to 2	$30	$30	0
6	five	$25	6 to 5	$30	$30	0
8	five	$25	6 to 5	$30	$30	0
9	four	$20	3 to 2	$30	$30	0
10	three	$15	2 to 1	$30	$30	0
Total: 24		$120	--------	$180	$180	0

Remember that in the oddsman bet, you can put what you like behind the Pass Line bet of another player.

Doey-Don't
(10 times odds)

#	Ways to make	Money at risk	True odds	Expected win	Actual win	Casino tax
4	three	$150	2 to 1	$300	$300	0
5	four	$200	3 to 2	$300	$300	0
6	five	$250	6 to 5	$300	$300	0
8	five	$250	6 to 5	$300	$300	0
9	four	$200	3 to 2	$300	$300	0
10	three	$150	2 to 1	$300	$300	0
minus one appearance of the 12 in 36 rolls					-$ 5	$5
Total: 24		$1,200	--------	$1,800	$1,795	$5

*The Come and Don't Come bets of five dollars each will cancel the other out and thus are not considered money-at-risk in the chart above. You will then place maximum odds of $50 on the Come portion of the bet to establish money-at-risk. However, we have to take into account the appearance of the 12 which will theoretically occur once in 36 perfect rolls, losing us five dollars.

Doey-Don't
(double odds)

#	Ways to make	Money at risk	True odds	Expected win	Actual win	Casino tax
4	three	$30	2 to 1	$60	$60	0
5	four	$40	3 to 2	$60	$60	0
6	five	$50	6 to 5	$60	$60	0
8	five	$50	6 to 5	$60	$60	0
9	four	$40	3 to 2	$60	$60	0
10	three	$30	2 to 1	$60	$60	0
minus one appearance of the 12 in 36 rolls					-$5	$5
Total: 24		$240	--------	$360 •	$355	$5

Pass Line or Come Bets
(10 times odds)

#	Ways to make	Money at risk	True odds	Expected win	Actual win	Casino tax
4	three	$165	2 to 1	$330	$315	$15
5	four	$220	3 to 2	$330	$320	$10
6	five	$275	6 to 5	$330	$325	$ 5
8	five	$275	6 to 5	$330	$325	$ 5
9	four	$220	3 to 2	$330	$320	$10
10	three	$165	2 to 1	$330	$315	$15
plus/minus come out wins*				--------	+$ 20	-$20
Total: 24		$1320	--------	$1980	$1940	$40

* Seven and 11 win eight times on come out rolls but two, three and 12 lose four times, thus a net win of four bets or $20 on come out rolls is added to the Actual win column and subtracted from the Casino tax column.

Pass Line or Come Bets
(double odds)

#	Ways to make	Money at risk	True odds	Expected win	Actual win	Casino tax
4	three	$45	2 to 1	$90	$75	$15
5	four	$60	3 to 2	$90	$80	$10
6	five	$75	6 to 5	$90	$85	$ 5
8	five	$75	6 to 5	$90	$85	$ 5
9	four	$60	3 to 2	$90	$80	$10
10	three	$45	2 to 1	$90	$75	$15
plus/minus come out wins					+ $20	-$20
Total: 24		$360	-------	$540	$500	$40

Traditional Place Betting

#	Ways to win	Money at risk	True odds	House odds	Expected win	Actual win	Casino tax
4	three	$30	2 to 1	9 to 5	$60	$54	$6
5	four	$40	3 to 2	7 to 5	$60	$56	$4
6	five	$60	6 to 5	7 to 6	$72	$70	$2
8	five	$60	6 to 5	7 to 6	$72	$70	$2
9	four	$40	3 to 2	7 to 5	$60	$56	$4
10	three	$30	2 to 1	9 to 5	$60	$54	$6
Total: 24		$260	-------	--------	$384	$360	$24

Note: this chart is based on placing the four, five, nine and 10 for $10 each, and placing the six and eight for $12 each. The six and eight must be placed in multiples of six dollars because of the seven to six payoff structure.

Best Buys Place Betting

The following chart is based upon buying the four and 10 for $39 and buying the five and nine for $38 and paying a one dollar tax each time these bets are placed. Also, I am assuming that you are a high roller and thus you are placing the six and eight for $60 each. If you are placing them for less, the percentages would be slightly different on the equalization tables.

#	Ways to make	Money at risk	True odds	House odds	Expected win	Actual win	Casino tax
4	three	$117	2 to 1	9 to 5	$234	$234	$3
5	four	$152	3 to 2	7 to 5	$228	$228	$4
6	five	$300	6 to 5	7 to 6	$360	$350	$10
8	five	$300	6 to 5	7 to 6	$360	$350	$10
9	four	$152	3 to 2	7 to 5	$228	$228	$4
10	three	$117	2 to 1	9 to 5	$234	$234	$3
minus total buys on four,five,nine, and 10						-$14	$34
Total: 24		$1138	-------	-------	$1644	$1610	$34

Equalization Table

This table is based on the assumption that you have won your bet. We wish to see how much of a tax the casinos take out of every $100 you would have won had the game been fair. A fair game is defined as one where neither the casino, nor the player, has the edge.

System of Betting	If you should have won...	Actual win	Casino Tax
Oddsman	$100	$100	0
Doey-Don't w/10X odds	$100	$99.72	28 cents
Doey-Don't double odds	$100	$98.61	$1.39
Pass Line/Come w/10X odds	$100	$97.98	$2.02
Best Buys Place Betting	$100	$97.93	$2.07
Traditional Place Betting	$100	$93.75	$6.25
Pass Line/Come double odds	$100	$92.59	$7.41

Crazy Crapper Bets

The following chart is based upon betting five dollars on the various propositions or hardways bets.

Individual Bets	You should have won...	Actual win	Casino tax
Any Seven	$25	$20	$5
Any Craps	$40	$35	$5
Two	$175	$150	$25
Twelve	$175	$150	$25
Three	$85	$75	$10
Eleven	$85	$75	$10
Hard four or ten	$40	$35	$5
Hard six or eight	$50	$45	$5
Big six or Big eight	$6	$5	$1
Field*	$100	$89.47	$10.53

*If you are placing bets in the Field consistently, if you should have won $100 in a fair game, you would only win $89.47 in a casino.

Paone Press
PO Box 610
Lynbrook, NY 11563

Paone Press proudly announces its lineup of great, new gaming publications with one purpose in mind - to make you a winner! *All prices already include two-day priority postage and handling.*

Chance and Circumstance - Frank Scoblete's quarterly newsletter of fact, opinion, analysis and inside information about this gaming life. It's all high-powered content and it's all about the chances we take - in a casino or in life - and the circumstances that we either take advantage of or that take advantage of us. Edited and written by gaming's premier writer, Frank Scoblete, *Chance and Circumstance* is the newsletter for the thinking man and woman. Whether you're a table-game player or an aficionado of slots or video poker, or just an observer of the passing casino and gaming scene, this is the newsletter for you. Commentary by the Captain. Best bets by John F. Julian. And no-nonsense, sharp-shooting advice on where to find the best games and the hottest machines.

"*Frank Scoblete will become to casino games what Hoyle was to games of cards: the authority to read on the subject!*"

...*Dr. Marvin Karlins, author and gaming columnist*

Subscribe today! One year is $50. Three years is $149 and your choice of any one of the following books free of charge. Five years is $189 and your choice of any two of the following books free of charge. Five year subscribers also receive a 25% discount on all future purchases from Paone Press during the lifetime of the subscription.

Guerrilla Gambling: How to Beat the Casinos at Their Own Games! by Frank Scoblete (published by Bonus Books $16.95)

"*Scoblete gives us a* tour de force *through the temples of chance. In precise, up-to-date and delightful prose, Frank Scoblete has done what no other gaming author has been able to do - in one volume - cover winning strategies, some quite radical, for almost every game, both old and new, the casinos offer. He even gives you a feeling for what it's like to gamble as he does. If you could read only one gaming book,* Guerrilla Gambling *would be my recommendation.*"

...*Dr. Marvin Karlins, author and gaming columnist*

"*Packed with new ideas and strategies. Written with insight, based on experienced play. A must read!*" ...*Howard Schwartz, Gambler's Book Club*

Julian's No-Nonsense Guide to Winning Blackjack by John F. Julian ($16.95). You can't beat today's blackjack games using yesterday's strategies. This book gives you up-to-date information on how to win in *today's* blackjack games. Includes the *Sprint Strategies* for multiple decks, the *Scan Techniques* for single decks; *basic strategy* and *card counting* for single and multiple decks; a basic strategy for *Double Exposure* and *Multiple Action* blackjack. Also includes the *Ultimate Blackjack Test!*

"*This book provides good, solid advice! Recommended!*"

...*Michael Dalton, Dalton's Blackjack Review*

The Julian Strategies in Roulette by John F. Julian ($16.95). At last, strategies geared to beating the wheel! Discover the difference between *layout strategies* and *wheel strategies* and how to win at both. Learn how to *bend the wheel to your will* by *Slicing the Pie, Looking for the Lucky Lady, Finding and Betting the BIG number!* An intelligent, clear and straightforward analysis of the game and how to beat it!

"*The best book on roulette!*" ...*Casino Player Magazine*

The Morons of Blackjack and Other Monsters by King Scobe [Frank Scoblete] ($16.95). There's more to playing blackjack than basic strategies and count systems. There's an emotional side. Let King Scobe, one of the finest blackjack players in the country and a writer of remarkable skill, take you on a journey into the mind, heart, and horrors of playing blackjack with morons and other monsters. Funny, sad, hard-hitting analysis of the people who play the game, and the casinos and personnel who offer it. A must read for anyone who enjoys going to casinos.

"*Once a player has mastered basic strategy...The Morons of Blackjack should be required reading!*" ...*letter to Dalton's Blackjack Review*

Beat the Craps Out of the Casinos: How to Play Craps and Win by Frank Scoblete (Published by Bonus Books: $13.95). Meet "the Captain," who has beaten the casinos since 1978 at a game players and pundits alike consider unbeatable. Learn how he does it! Explore the Captain's revolutionary methods of play: *the 5-Count, the Supersystem, Pushing the House,* as well as information on *money management* and the *mental edge.* Filled with insight, advice, and wonderful stories about the Captain and his legendary *Crew* of high rollers.

"*Scoblete has done it! Surprisingly new ideas. Informative and entertaining for both the novice and hardcore shooter!*"

...*Howard Schwartz, the Gambler's Book Club*

The Captain's Craps Revolution by Frank Scoblete ($21.95). The war against the casinos has begun. This book is for serious craps players who wish to fully explore the Captain's revolutionary methods of play: the *5-Count*, the *Classic Supersystem* and the *Radical Supersystem.* For the first time ever, you'll learn about two *new "buy" bets* that radically reduce the house advantage, and a method of playing that *totally wipes out* the house's mathematical edge! This book offers unique insights into the game, the nature of chance and randomness, table selection, controlling and fixing the dice, and how to get comped while playing a variation of the *Supersystem.*

"Frank Scoblete is a player, theorist and author and he writes for the person who wants to take home the money!"
...Howard Schwartz, the Gambler's Book Club

Break the One-Armed Bandits by Frank Scoblete (published by Bonus Books $13.95) The breakthrough book that reveals for the first time ever from an *inside* source exactly where the "loose" and "tight" machines are located in a casino! From the birth of the slots in the 1890's to the creation of today's new "smart machines," everything you ever wanted to know about the slots is in this book. Frank Scoblete explains how the machines, both old and new, work - and how to beat them! You'll learn expert strategies and money-management systems that are geared to s-t-r-e-t-c-h-i-n-g your time at the machines but not your risk.

"Frank Scoblete's book is a must for the expert or rookie player. It is delightfully entertaining and insightful. He offers informative ways to attack the machines and avoid the traps of slot play. He has a humorous and easy-to-read style. Great reading!"
...Jim Hildebrand, columnist, Casino Player Magazine

All prices already include two-day priority postage and handling!

Three and five year subscribers to **Chance and Circumstance**, *remember to order your free books!*